Seductio Ad Absurdum

The Principles & Practices of Seduction, A Beginner's Handbook

Emily Hahn

Originally Published by
BREWER AND WARREN INC. / PAYSON & CLARKE LTD.
1930

Contents

WHAT IS SEDUCTION?   3
    SEDUCTION IN HISTORY 6

THIS MODERN WORLD   9
    DIFFICULTIES OF RESEARCH 9
    METHOD OF TREATMENT 11

1. I THINK YOU HAVE A GREAT CAPACITY FOR LIVING   13

2. JUST ANOTHER LITTLE ONE   17

3. FEEL MY MUSCLE   21

4. YOU'RE NOT THE DOMESTIC TYPE   25

5. I'M BAD   29

6. AN UGLY OLD THING LIKE ME   33

7. BE INDEPENDENT!   37

8. WHAT DO YOU THINK YOUR HUSBAND'S DOING?   41

9. MUSIC GETS ME   47

10. EVERYBODY DOES   51

11. THIS BUSINESS   55

12. GAME LITTLE KID   59

13. PROMISE ME YOU WON'T   63

14. AH, WHAT IS LIFE?   67

15. A MAN MY AGE	71
16. GONNA BE NICE?	77
17. LIFE IS SHORT	81
18. I'D HAVE SAID YOU WERE FROM NEW YORK	85
19. SHE LOVED ME FOR THE DANGERS	91
BIBLIOGRAPHY	95

SEDUCTIO AD ABSURDUM
("Now I lay me—"
OLD PRAYER)
DEDICATED TO
HERBERT ASBURY
WHO TOLD ME TO WRITE IT DOWN
INTRODUCTION

Although seduction as an applied art has been slowly developing over a period of several generations, the science of seduction has so far been largely neglected. While the value of the empirical knowledge acquired by early practitioners and transmitted to us by a great body of folk-lore should not be minimized, the trial and error methods of these precursors, both amateur and professional, are to be deplored as crude; for however refined they may have been in application, there is evidence that they were lacking in that exactness in observation which could make them valuable to science.

Only a very few though hardy pioneers have in the past, recognized the necessity for organizing man's empirical knowledge of this vast subject on a rational basis, and it is due to their unselfish labours alone that we now have a sufficient body of observed phenomena, a sufficient accumulation of data, to make possible the beginnings of a true science of seduction. It is the purpose of this book, to co-ordinate the efforts of these for the most part anonymous and forgotten contributors, these modest, silent benefactors, and to attempt a proper classification within the subject: to adumbrate such practical methods of procedure as may in the, let us hope, near future develop into a sure technique. Owing to the limitations of space and the present confused state of the subject, it is of necessity only possible here to indicate the lines which such a development must follow. It is my desire to confine this work to a purely practical consideration of the subject, and to make it a handbook in the hope that my students and those who come after me will be the better able to add to the body of our observed knowledge of seduction and to indicate the more clearly for my shortcomings along what lines improvement is required.

WHAT IS SEDUCTION?

In the first place, the word itself is unfortunately obscure, possessing an ambiguity which we must resolve before we can proceed. I have assembled an assortment of representative definitions, which follows:

Se-duce (se-dus) v.t.; SE-DUCED (se-dust); SE-DUCING (-dusing). [L. seducere, seductum; se-aside—ducere to lead. See DUKE.] I. To lead aside or astray, esp. from the path of rectitude or duty; to entice to evil; to corrupt.

"For me, the gold of France did not seduce."
—Shakespeare
—Webster's New International Dictionary

Seduce, v.t. Lead astray, tempt into sin or crime, corrupt; persuade (woman) into surrender of chastity, debauch.
—Concise Oxford Dictionary

Seduire: v.a. (du lat. seducere, conduire à l'écart. Se conj. comme conduire). Faire tomber en erreur ou en faute par ses insinuations, ses exemples.
—Larousse

Seduccion: Acciôn y effecto de seducir.
Seducfr: Engañar con are y maña, persuadir suavemente al mal.
—Enciclopedia Universal Illustrada.

Sedurre (Seduzione, n) Ridurre con vane o false apparenze al nostre valere e al male.
—Dizionario Universale delta Lingua Italiana. Petrocchi

Verfiihrung; in geschlechtlicher Beziehung ein Mädchen verführen.
—Deutsches Wörterbuch ... Heynes

It is obvious that these interpretations all suffer from a common fault: they fail to reflect the modern ramifications of the word. As a matter of fact, seduction is undergoing a great change.

The rudiments of the custom may be observed in the remnants of primitive society that we are able to study. Certain aboriginal tribes practise polyandry as an economic adjustment to the surplus of males.[1] With the development of civilization we find that adaptation tends to take the form of matriarchy, as in the United States.[2]

In the early days of our culture, seduction was practised upon certain species of recognized placer in the social system, and thus attained a certain grade of standardization. There were the seduced (always the feminine sex) and the seducers (masculine). It would appear that with the aforementioned rise of matriarchy this state of affairs is changing. The predatory instinct of humanity is not confined to the male. However, the line of reasoning suggested is too vast to follow in the limits of a small volume, and I mention it merely that the student may think about it at his leisure as he peruses the forthcoming chapters.

The extraordinary development of prostitution in the nineteenth century prefaced the present phase with a last manifestation of the old social attitude. Relying upon the assumption that the male seduces the female, we are faced in this modern world with the undeniable fact that the ranks of the seduced— i.e., the unprotected young women of society—are also shifting and changing. The orderly arrangement which we have been led to expect is breaking up. In former times our women were divided into two main classes, or groups:

(a) Professionals (those who made a vocation of being seduced)[3]

(b) Amateurs (those to whom the process of being seduced was a side line).[4]

However in late years there has grown up among us a third class, designated as (c), The only familiar term which has yet been applied was coined by Doctor Ethel Waters, who invented for them the descriptive appellation "freebies" in recognition of their independent stand in the matter of economics and convention. These revolutionists have formulated a philosophy which draws upon those of both older classes for its sources. To be freebie, seduction is neither a means of livelihood, as in the case of class (a), nor inevitable disgrace, as it is with class (b).[5]

It is undoubtedly this school of thought that influenced the Missouri jurist who, after a long and tiresome case of seduction, in which he found for the defendant, made a pronouncement from the bench to the effect that "There is no such thing as seduction."[6] Although in my opinion this statement is somewhat extreme for our purposes, it serves to demonstrate the modern trend of sentiment.[7]

The modern social attitude had its prototype in the days of Cleopatra, where, as every classical scholar knows, the women of the upper classes exhibited an amazing independence. In Rome and Alexandria "the professional courtesans were gloomily complaining that their business had been hard hit by the fact that the ladies of fashion asked no payment for exertions of a similar nature."[8]

Taking these facts into consideration, we must admit that in the light of modern improvement a new definition is required: one more in line with present day practice. For the purpose of this treatise let it be understood therefore that seduction is the process of persuading someone to do that which he or she has wanted to do all the time.

[1]

The Sexual Life of Savages. B. Malinowski.

[2]

Domestic Manners of the Americans. By Frances Trollope. New York; Dodd, Mead and Company, 1927.

[3]

Recreations of a Merchant, or the Christian Sketch Book. By William A. Brewer. Boston. See also Hatrack by Herbert Asbury, The American Mercury, April, 1926; and The Brass Check. By Upton Sinclair. Pasadena.

[4]

The Beautiful Victim: Being a Full Account of the Seduction and Sorrows of Miss Mary Kirkpatrick (National Police Gazette: 1862).

[5]

The Green Hat. By Michael Arlen.

[6]

Eddinger versus Thompson: Harris j.

[7]

For further exposition of juridical aspects of the subject see Die Zivilrechtlichen Ansprüche von Frauenspersonen aus aus-serehelichem Beischlafe: Hans Hochstein.

[8]

Personalities of Antiquity ... Arthur Weigall.

SEDUCTION IN HISTORY

The records preserved from older civilizations are (as has been said before) too fundamental in treatment to be of much value to us in the matter of details. We know, however, that the mythology and folklore of any race presents a more or less accurate idea of the customs of the time. Granting an amount of exaggeration in the fables, we have still the proof that seduction has always been a recognized practice in Heaven. Scarcely a god has not dabbled in the art at one time or another. In the first place they start off with the advantages of divinity and a working knowledge of black magic.[9] They could be called seducers in the true sense of the word only by courtesy. Jupiter, to take an example, used methods of archaic and brutal simplicity. To be sure, he would sometimes take the trouble to turn himself into a swan or a bull or a shower of gold, but such exercises are second nature to a deity and cause no delay or exhaustion. Ammon, the Egyptian god, associated exclusively with royalty, and no one thought of calling him to task for such moral irregularities. On the contrary, the kingly family was proud of him.[10]

A close study of the ancient Indians reveals the fact that they deemed seduction one of the most important of the arts, rivalling philosophy in popularity as a study.[11] The Chinese with their customary reserve, make no mention of such matters in official papers, but a quantity of poetry and maxims discloses a keen Oriental interest in the topic.[12] The Old Testament abounds in stories of seduction by means of trickery, bribery and simple persuasion. It is safe to assume from the records that seduction in all parts of the civilized world was at about the same stage of primary development.

The Middle Ages show some progress. Literature was growing into an important culture, and we have much more source material. There are manifestations of refinement in the ancient game, but at the same time the world was not as light-hearted about these matters as it had been in the past. The growth of the Church, with its set ideas of these subjects and its zeal to catalogue the sins of mankind and to deal out punishment accordingly, gave to seduction its greatest impetus. At no other time in history has such a vast amount of time and thought been expended on one idea. It became a sin, and therefore a necessity.

Added to the stimulation of the churchly attitude was that of the caste system, which made seduction the only means of communication between the classes. The Renaissance introduced a new fashion, persuasion by means of bribery. Kings and their courtiers led the movement by elevating their mistresses to dizzy heights of power and wealth. The sixteenth, seventeenth and eighteenth centuries witnessed an influx of new families and the ascent of many a lowly maiden. Several of the noblest families of England trace their origin to such glittering seductions.[13] Indeed this process became at one time so notorious that it crept into folklore and has been preserved for us in

many a ballad, of which the following is representative:
"She was poor but she was honest,
Victim of the Squire's whim."
Even before this period, England had introduced a variation of the art in the form of Chivalry. This school of behaviour, while professing an ignorance of the very rudiments of seduction, nevertheless played an important part in its development, as is convincingly illustrated by the old song:
"In days of old, when knights were bold
And barons held their sway,
A warrior bold, with spurs of gold,
Sang merrily his lay."
But aside from the royal habits, there was no imagination, no finesse to seduction. It was a stereotyped affair, a furtive irregularity, a silly little sin. The seduction of the middle classes was a monotonous business, popular only by reason of the danger it entailed. It has remained for our modern world to raise it to a place of dignity among the leading interests of all society.

[9]

Bulfinch's Mythology.

[10]

The Golden Bough. Sir J. Frazer.

[11]

The Kama Sutra.

[12]

Colored Stars. E. Powys Mathers. Houghton Mifflin.

[13]

Cf. The Complete Peerage.

THIS MODERN WORLD

What are the reasons for this recent tendency? There are many answers. In the first place, mankind need no longer turn the whole of its energy to defence and sustenance. The life of the average man is not completely devoted to his business. He is a rarely active person if one-third of his day is given over to actual work.

"I work eight hours, I sleep eight hours,
That leaves eight hours for love."
—Popular ballad
Otherwise what does he do with his time?
"What makes the business man tired?
What does the business man do?"
—Popular song

He reads, he plays, sometimes he wages war, and for the rest of the time he sleeps, eats and makes love. We find ourselves in a restless age, a time of experiment; when almost everyone is urged by the same desire to revise and improve.

It is the Golden Age of good living, consequently it is the age of impending boredom. In such an atmosphere we would expect to find a development of parlour pastimes. These conditions, this pleasant leisure, this much vaunted, generally diffused prosperity, this impatience for hallowed tradition and the time-honoured devices for improving one's time, have given rise to crossword puzzles, introspection, and modern seduction.

DIFFICULTIES OF RESEARCH

Since the connotation of the word has been altered, I venture to assert that there have been converted to the practices of seduction at least twice as many devotees as had flourished before. This statement will undoubtedly be challenged: once more, I make no doubt, the skeptical will object to my conclusions on the grounds that a scientific recluse is of necessity withdrawn from the world and its customs and is thus automatically excluded as a responsible judge of sociological problems. It might be appropriate in this preface to enter a plea for our great body of research workers who are submitted to this sort of amateur criticism. The path of the scientist is beset with difficulties of every nature; not only those in the natural line of his work, but the wholesale hostility of the uninformed layman who does not understand the hardships and delays of laboratory procedure. In this case I hope to forestall criticism by claiming to have followed a conscientious program of newspaper reading. My statement is based on the knowledge common to the layman. I cite as proof the columns of the newspapers, both the items of fact and the syndicated columns which, it would appear, devote seventy-five per cent of their space to discussion of the present generation and what to do about it.

Indeed other students of society have gone farther, much farther. Dr. Henry W. Gardner, eminent social psychologist, seven years ago devoted his doctor's thesis to the so-called conditions of morality then prevailing on the "campus." With highly commendable enthusiasm, this scholar spent almost the entire school year in an alder bush that grew on the edge of a secluded path known to irreverent minds as Lover's Lane, where the youths of the university were wont to take their evening strolls. He adduced the following significant statistics:

Of the 3,061 automobiles that drove through the lane in one week, 2,009 stopped, and 2,005 turned off the motors. Of these, 154 drove on again after periods of time varying to an upper limit of five minutes. Of the remainder, 1,788 parked for periods of not less than one hour and not more than two hours and three-quarters. Dr. Gardner ascribed the fixation of these limits to the period between the beginning of darkness (which of course varied with the season) and the "coeds'" curfew.

Of the remaining sixty-three, forty-nine of the automobiles spent the entire night in the lane. The fate of the other fourteen will never be known: they were all still there on the historic night when a watchman stumbled over Dr. Gardner's feet and took him to jail before he could explain. The vicissitudes and obstacles that stand in the scientist's way cannot be overestimated. This deplorable incident is merely one example of the prevalent attitude.

Another of his experiments was to fix a dictaphone beneath the old oak bench at the far end of Lover's Lane. He did this shortly after the unfortunate episode of the jail, and for eleven nights he was thus enabled to sit at his ease in the laboratory, taking notes. (I myself have much reason to thank and commend Dr. Gardner's foresight: these notes, while they have not been used as source material, have nevertheless allowed me to corroborate many of my own conclusions.)

METHOD OF TREATMENT

The method used in this treatise is the result of much thought. After attempting several other outlines, I have come to the conclusion that the most graphic representation is that of hypothetical cases for each lesson—i.e., each chapter represents a typical case, or synthetic experience. The student may at first glance object to this treatment, but a short survey will, I hope, convince him that the system is the only adequate one possible. Note that each experiment is couched in colloquial terms, the better to carry the atmosphere of the lesson. Of course the student is expected to vary the program according to his own requirements: these experiments are to serve merely as outlines. I have attempted to avoid as far as possible that wealth of technical terminology so dear to the heart of the average scientific author and so trying to the beginner: I have dared to hope that my compilation would be an aid not only to that small band who have dedicated their lives exclusively to research, but also to the great masses, the dilettantes and amateurs who might be able to find some inspiration in these pages.

The preparation, both research and field work, has been arduous, but what accomplishment was ever valuable without some labour and pains? If my contribution to scientific literature has in some small measure advanced the penetration of my fellow man and eased his path of loving, I am amply repaid.

In conclusion, I wish to thank those who have worked with me. Without their unfailing patience, sympathy and assiduity this little book could never have been written.

New York.
Thanksgiving, 1929.
E. H.
EXPERIMENTS
WHAT IS SEDUCTION?
THIS MODERN WORLD
CHAPTER
I THINK YOU HAVE A GREAT CAPACITY FOR LIVING
JUST ANOTHER LITTLE ONE
FEEL MY MUSCLE
YOU'RE NOT THE DOMESTIC TYPE
I'M BAD
AN UGLY OLD THING LIKE ME
BE INDEPENDENT!
WHAT DO YOU THINK YOUR HUSBAND'S DOING?
MUSIC GETS ME
EVERYBODY DOES
THIS BUSINESS

GAME LITTLE KID
PROMISE ME YOU WON'T
AH, WHAT IS LIFE?
A MAN MY AGE
GONNA BE NICE?
LIFE IS SHORT
I'D HAVE SAID YOU WERE FROM NEW YORK
SHE LOVED ME FOR THE DANGERS

BIBLIOGRAPHY

1. I THINK YOU HAVE A GREAT CAPACITY FOR LIVING

TYPE:
Well-to-do man with slightly artistic tendencies; the sort that believes first in money, then in full enjoyment of it. His philosophy is practical but not too limited to material considerations; in other words, he talks well on almost any subject.

SUBJECT:
Slightly younger, but of the same breed. The families of the two protagonists have probably been friendly for two generations.

APPARATUS:
A restaurant: one of the more leisurely ones where the dishes do not rattle but an orchestra makes conversation just as difficult.

REMARKS:
The keynote of the approach is a tacit appreciation of intelligence on the part of the subject. This sympathetic attitude is very important. Think it all over carefully, put a flower in your buttonhole and go ahead.

I THINK YOU HAVE A GREAT CAPACITY FOR LIVING

You have reached the coffee and are putting up a brave fight against the orchestra before going out into the privacy of the street.

She: And we didn't get home, after all, until two o'clock. I was so angry: it spoiled the evening.

You: Angry! I don't think that you could ever be angry.

She: Oh, yes, you don't know me at all. I have a dreadful temper.

You: Well, it doesn't somehow fit in with my idea of you, you see. No, I must disagree with you. You haven't a temper. It's impossible for you to have a really earthly emotion.

She (somewhat irritated): Why, how can you say such a thing?

You: You're a strangely aloof child, you know.

She (after a pleased little silence): That's not nice of you.

You: Why not? It's so nice of you, you know.

She: Oh, do you really think so? I'm sure I don't try to be. No.... (with a charming smile)—you're quite wrong. It's the rest of them that are different. I'm really very normal.

You: Normal? Oh, my dear! And yet, after all, it's not very funny. Perhaps it's a tragedy.

She: What is?

You: Your attitude toward life.

She: Why, I have no attitude!

You: There you are; that's just it. Someone of us mortals tries to tell you how we—how flesh-and-blood beings react to you, and you simply open those clear eyes of yours, and—well, how can I go on talking in the face of such bland ignorance?

She: Ignorance! Why I don't....

You: Oh, surely you know how ignorant you are? You must remain ignorant with deliberation. It's part of your charm, of course, but ... oh, how charming you could be, in another way!

She: Really.... (suddenly her voice warms and she leans a little over the table, talking eagerly) No, you're perfectly right. I mean from your viewpoint, of course. One thing that you forget, though, is that I don't feel the way that you and the rest of them do. I can't really understand it myself, and yet ... oh, all that sort of thing; emotion and all that; seems so ... so messy.

You: Messy? My dear child, what sort of people can you have known?

She: Perfectly normal people, I assure you. No, it's my own fault. It's me, and I can't help it. Emotion to me has always seemed—no thank you, just demi-tasse—seemed common. Not aristocratic. That's rather a snide thing to say, isn't it? I don't mean to sound that way.

You: I know you don't. (The music plays without competition for a moment). But how sad!

She: Sad? Oh no. I get along quite well. I'm really very happy, except once in a while. I'm as happy, that is, as you can possibly be for all your—your normality.

You: But what a strange way for an intelligent person like yourself to think! Have you no curiosity?

She: Oh, certainly. To an extent. But when curiosity conflicts with one's disgusts....

You: Disgusts? Now you are certainly wrong. It gives you away.

She: Yes, that was a silly thing to say.

You: Don't you think that you allow your mind to rule you too much? It's really dangerous. I mean it. Surely your intelligence tells you that a well-rounded personality....

She: But I told you; I don't want to experiment!

You: I can't believe that you are in a position to judge. You don't really know what you want; you don't know what to want. I don't believe you for a minute when you say you are happy. Lovely, yes; but lovely in a melancholy way. How can you know about yourself, you wise child? Tell me, are you always so serene?

She: You're getting much too serious. Let's dance.

You: I don't want to dance with you just now. I think you're trying to run away from me as you have always run away from questions. Do you know, you're a most deceptive person. When I met you, I said to myself, "She is sensitive," but I never thought of you as being beautiful. I'm being frank, do you mind? But I see now that you are. I see that you are rarely beautiful, but that you do not wish to be. Isn't that true?

She: Why no, of course not. I don't understand it all.

You: It's just this, and I don't care whether or not I offend you. In fact, I hope I do. Someone ought to offend you now and then. You're committing a crime, not only against us but against yourself. If I had my way—and I'm not being selfish, either—

She (blazing): As though any of you weren't selfish!

You: What?

She: I'm so tired of it all. Don't you think I hear something like this every day of my life? All of you working for yourselves, arguing for yourselves, talking eternally about the same thing. I can't stand any more of it. I'm sick of it.

You (gravely): I beg your pardon, but you're not being quite polite, are you? You're a bit unjust.

She: Perhaps I'm rather excited. Sorry.

You: Perhaps not. This is the result of a long silence, isn't it? You have never spoken like this before?

She: Yes, that's it.

You (leaning forward): My dear, if I've said anything....

She (faintly): No, it's nothing. Tell me, how can you—all of you—be so cold blooded and unfastidious at the same time?

You: Oh, but you are wrong. I'm sure that as a rule we are more fastidious than you could possibly know. I'm sorry that I've disturbed you—Check, please! I'm going to take you home.

She: No, I was foolish. You're right. I'm sure you're right. But I couldn't help it. Have I hurt you?

You: Let's forget it all. Let's go somewhere and talk about other things. (You rise and start to the door.) I didn't want to spoil the evening, much as you seemed to think so. Should we go to my place and look at the print I just bought? It's so early to take you home.

She: Yes, that would be nice.

You: There, you see; I've done you an injustice. You're quite human underneath it all. Probably someone has hurt you, and you won't tell me about it. I think, my dear, that you have a very great capacity for living. Let's take one with the top down. TAXI!!

2. JUST ANOTHER LITTLE ONE

TYPE:

Virile, young, simple. A man who does not waste time on philosophical reflections; who knows what he wants and stops at nothing but sacrifice to get it.

SUBJECT:

Very young, semi-sophisticated. That is, she has been warned but not insulated.

APPARATUS:

1 Victrola

1 Radio

1 Bottle Scotch

1 Automobile

1 House—Anybody's

1 Party

REMARKS:

The inclusion in the collection of this lesson is accompanied by some misgivings on my part. It is a method of which we do not approve. The true seduction does not depend upon mechanical devices such as alcohol. I counsel my students to save this method until all else fails, for it leads to a slackness and a lazy attitude toward the work. Moreover, it is against the law in this country to buy liquor or to carry it around.

JUST ANOTHER LITTLE ONE

> The introduction. Give everyone full notice, but when her name is mentioned, employ the personal touch in your bow—the lingering glance shading off in friendly admiration.
>
> Wait half an hour, perhaps employing the time with a drink. Dance with everyone else and be looking at her twice when she glances your way.
>
> Suddenly walking over to her, you should look accusingly at the half-full glass in her hand.

"You don't mean to tell me that's your first?"

"Yes."

"Say, who are you anyway? Have I ever seen you around?"

"No, Joe and Edna brought me. I don't know anyone here very well."

"Who's Joe?"

"The little fellow over there."

"Your heavy?"

"Silly! No, of course not. He and Edna just got married. That's why they're having this party, isn't it?"

"I don't know. I was invited, that's all I know. Well, see you later."

Get up and go away at this point; too much at first is too much.

Soon after this it is likely that the lady will finish her glass mechanically; and the next one will go down with more alacrity. Keep an eye on her, and when she has finished the second one come back and ask her to dance. If you are a good dancer the whole thing is easier, but so few of you are.

Put her down when it is over, smile at her politely and go away again. This mystifies her.

Two drinks later. Don't drink too much; this requires as much concentration as any other business. It's time now to focus the attack.

After two or three dances the room seems uncomfortably warm, and now that she is accustomed to being monopolized she won't be averse to stepping outdoors with you to get cool. Any car will do if it is unoccupied.

There will be a slightly awkward pause; breathless and afraid on her part. Then she realizes that your intentions are all right and she is ashamed of her own suspicions.

"My, but it must have been warm in there," she says. "I didn't realize it. What a lovely night!"

"Yeah, the gang's crazy to stay indoors in this weather.... Say, what do you do all the time? I haven't seen you around."

"Well, I haven't been in town very long. I'm visiting Edna."

"Having a good time?"

"Oh, yes. Everyone's been so nice to me."

"Naturally they would be, to you. I guess you have a pretty good time wherever you go."

"Aw, that's an old one!"

"You don't swallow everything you hear, do you? Well, that's right." ... a burst of music comes through the window ... "Say, I've got a drink or two here. Want one?"

"Oh no—I've had enough. But you go right ahead."

"Nope, I don't drink without company."

"Well—just a little one."

2. JUST ANOTHER LITTLE ONE 19

After the bottle has been tucked away again, settle down with a deep sigh and put your arm around her. While she's wondering if she ought to let it stay there, turn around and pull her head over to yours, very lazily and comfortably.

"No! Please."
"All right."

Release her, avoiding all trace of petulance. She can think that over for a while.

After a long time, reach for the bottle again.

"Just another little one?"
Of course she doesn't want to be a complete prig—
"All right. But aren't you drinking a lot?"
"No. I never take too much."

There really isn't much to say. You don't want conversation; she knows you don't. She does—or does she? She doesn't know what she wants, just now. You've flustered her and upset her and started her thinking and you aren't doing anything to help her out. She wonders why you don't say something. She can't think of anything to say. She's thinking too hard of something which you have evidently forgotten. It is almost a relief when you put your arm around her again. Something definite, anyway. Even when you kiss her she doesn't protest. She thinks that it wasn't bad anyway; in fact it was a nice kiss—not too long nor too enthusiastic.

And as a matter of fact, this particular subject should not be a connoisseur of kisses. She would like to discuss it. Whenever she has been kissed before, the occasion seemed more momentous, with prelude of conversation and aftermath of protestation. Your absolute indifference intrigues her. You've evidently forgotten all about it already.

And then you yawn. Yawn and burrow your head in her breast in an affectionate, friendly manner; dropping off to sleep immediately. She sits very still and straight, hoping that you'll wake up, hoping you won't, hoping no one is watching you from the porch, wondering why she isn't objecting, wondering why she should, wondering about life in general.... It's all because she drank so much of that whiskey. She really doesn't feel so well. Sort of mixed up. Why don't you wake up? She wants to go in and dance; it must be late. How did this get started anyway?

She stirs a little at last, for her arm is going to sleep, and this wakes you. Open your eyes and pull her face down to yours—it's the most natural thing to do under the circumstances. "Sweet thing."

She is reassured. You are thinking of her, then. You've become once more a person, a man, instead of an abstract problem. And she knows how to deal with people, even with men. It's this other thing that worries her; this horrible impersonal wondering; this feeling of enmity that lurks in the air when people forget you and go to sleep. Although she couldn't put it into words....

2. JUST ANOTHER LITTLE ONE

"Another drink, sweet thing?"

"I guess so."

"Sure, just another little one now."

She isn't thinking at all now. If she were she'd probably suggest going in, for it is late and she wants to dance. But it doesn't seem late; it doesn't seem as though time is going on at all. She isn't thinking. She doesn't start to think even when you kiss her more enthusiastically and not so lazily. This must be the way a plant feels on a hot summer day when it hasn't anything to do but grow. Not happy; not sad.

It is only when she realized at last that you are growing importunate that she stirs herself and protests. She isn't sure what to say; the protest is more a matter of habit than anything else…. Everything is a habit…. And once more, for the last time, you say "Yes. One more. Just another little one."

3. FEEL MY MUSCLE

TYPE:
The man of action, of firm convictions and a limited sympathy for anyone who does not agree with him. Timid or sickly persons are advised to avoid this method.
SUBJECT:
An old-fashioned girl, apt to get a thrill when forcibly reminded of her comparative weakness.
APPARATUS:
1 Bathing Beach
1 Life-saving Uniform
2 Hot Dogs
REMARKS:
We all have some primitive instincts, even now. A crude exhibition of brute strength is fascinating to most of us, deny it as we will. The psychological basis for the reaction of the subject is probably a feeling that she will not have to bear the responsibility for whatever may happen.
FEEL MY MUSCLE
The holiday crowd is thinning out. Dusk shrouds the less decorative elements of the beach—the ragged holes left by children and the empty, soiled paper lunch boxes. Those revelers who are left see only the long curving line of the shore and a mysterious intermittent foaming as the lazy waves crash slowly against the sand.

Eloise lounges on the beach, watching the slow ebb of the Sunday gaiety. She thinks vaguely of going in for one more dip before she gets dressed; thinks of the shock of cold water on her already-dry bathing suit; thinks of the damp, dank-smelling dressing-room, and decides to postpone the whole thing for a few minutes. There is no hurry and she isn't cold. She runs her hand through her fuzzy hair and yawns. She is a slim girl with a slightly bored expression, and she is younger than she looks.

It has been a pleasant Sunday, withal rather dull. She hasn't come to the beach alone; she and the other file-clerk in the office have ventured out together. But Bessie has met up with a boy-friend and disappeared. Eloise does not hold a grudge against her for her desertion; it is understood that such accidents are likely to happen on Sunday afternoon. But she surveys the long lonely ride home with distaste. She chews her wad of Juicy Fruit dreamily and gives to the ukelele clutched to her diaphragm a pensive plunk.

It is at this moment that you sight her. You are strolling along the beach on your way in, after an arduous day of life-saving. Not that anyone has needed his life saved, but three blondes and two brunettes have required swimming lessons and all of them have been plump. By this time you prefer them slender; all the ladies tattooed on your arms are very slender indeed; and two of them wear red bathing-suits of the same shade as Eloise's. You stop short when you see her and wonder if you haven't seen her before somewhere. You decide that you haven't; and regret the fact. You wonder if she has noticed you. If she has, she doesn't show it. Not a missed beat has interrupted the mastication of her chewing-gum.

True to your vocation, adopt a nautical method of approach. In other words, tack. First walk along a line inclined at forty-five degrees to the most direct approach to Eloise. Somewhere at her right pause suddenly and examine a sand-crab. Then look up quickly, obviously under the impression that someone is calling you. After carefully looking at everything else on the beach, drop your eyes to Eloise, who blinks and turns away.

Sigh loudly and drop heavily and prone on the sand near her feet. Startled, she looks at you again. Grin and flip a pebble at her.

"Say!" says Eloise, indignantly.

"What do you say, girlie?" you counter. Then raise yourself in sections and redrape your lean length on the log next to her. "Ain't you lonesome?" you add.

It is a rhetorical question purely, but she does not want to play. She chooses to take you literally.

"Not much," she retorts. "I'm waiting for a guy."

Answer promptly, "Not any more, you ain't."

She compresses her lips and ignores you, fingering the strings of the ukelele in an abstracted way. It has no effect. Pat her arm and say:

"Give us a tune, kid?"

"Fresh!" she says scornfully. "Who you crowding?"

"Aw, don't be mean," you plead. "Give us a tune."

Eloise shakes her head quickly and decisively. "I didn't ask you over!" she reminds you. It is a warning that she is on her guard; that she is a difficult proposition; that she is a Nice Girl.

"Well, gee, can't a guy try to be human?" Your voice should be petulant and youthful. "I was just trying to be human. I was lonesome." It is a plaintive speech, and you look plaintive. But nevertheless you are a masculine being, strong and undefeated. Probably it is the bathing suit, or perhaps the air with which you light your cigarette. Eloise gazes at your profile in uncertainty. End the pause by casting away the match and turning to her.

3. FEEL MY MUSCLE

"So when I seen you I couldn't help talking. If you don't like it I'll go away. I got my pride, too."

This is a little better. "Oh, well, if you didn't mean to be fresh. You know a girl has got to be careful."

"Sure," you say, nodding. "I bet you do, all right."

"What do you mean?"

"Aw, you know what I mean!" say to her ardently. "Anybody ever tell you your eyes are pretty?"

"Fresh!" She starts picking at the ukelele again, slightly confused.

"Come on now, babe," you plead again. "Give us a tune."

"I don't know anything new," she apologizes in advance. "Do you know that one 'I Can't Give You Anything But Love'?"

"Go ahead," you murmur.

She plays the song, and then another, and another. The sun approaches the horizon and the ocean turns dark and green.

"Gee," says Eloise in low tones, "I got to go."

"Wait a minute, babe." Stand up and rumple her hair affectionately before leaving. Eloise shrouds herself in her bathrobe and waits. Presently you come back through the night, carrying two hot-dogs dripping mustard.

"Surround that," you order, proffering one. "It's a swell night. Anybody worrying about you? You cold?"

She shakes her head hesitantly. "N-no. But I'll have to go soon; it's awfully late."

You munch hungrily while the breeze dies down over the water. Then shift, disposing yourself more comfortably, and grunt contentedly. Eloise gives the head in her lap a little push, but it rolls back. She decides to ignore it.

"Gosh," you say at last, "a night like this is enough to make anybody feel soft. Even a guy like me."

"Yeah, I bet you're a hard guy!" she cries.

Lift your head and prop it on your hand. "Say, listen, babe! Anybody who says I ain't, don't know me! Does anybody ever bother you? Some of these drugstore sheiks ever get fresh?"

She hangs her head. "Well...."

"Well," cut her short, "if they do, send 'em around!" Make your voice ominous. "Don't let anybody tell you different. Look here." Raise your arm and clench your fist. "Feel that. There."

Eloise puts out a tentative and timid finger. "Ooo!" she cries. "Yes, I guess you could hit. I guess I wouldn't ever try to get you sore!"

"Baby," murmur tenderly, "you couldn't get me sore if you tried. I knew the minute I seen you you was a sweet kid. If anybody ever bothers you again, tell me. A nice kid like you hadn't ought to go around without somebody taking care of you. I remember once...." Here you stop. Somewhere down the beach another ukelele plays softly. You sigh and grope through the dark. She tries futilely to dislodge you.

"I really got to be going," she protests, somewhat frightened. She is always somewhat frightened when the fellows get too fresh.

"Now listen, babe. You ain't afraid of me, You needn't be. Don't go away yet; you're all right. Just a little longer." And yet, as before, for all your pleading tones there should be a hint of strength in your speech. Eloise yields, but whether to your imploring or your strength she does not know.

"Well," she says, "if you're nice."

Silence lives on the beach, except for the tiny wailing of the ukelele. Silently the water undulates and the moon creeps over the edge of it.

"Quit it!" says Eloise, giggling nervously. Do not answer. "Aw, quit!" Still you do not answer. "Please! You're too strong. Oh, quit!"

The other ukelele still plays, spreading over the night a sweet layer of romance; singing of exotic love on a whiter, warmer beach in a more delicate world; singing of love, as though love were a thing to be sung.

4. YOU'RE NOT THE DOMESTIC TYPE

TYPE:
The sensitive young man with a predilection for virtuous married women. Charmingly impetuous.
SUBJECT:
A virtuous married woman.
APPARATUS:
1 Living room
1 Chaise-longue
REMARKS:
Love, maternal instinct and pity are all emotions that should be employed in this lesson, but the most important factor of all is spirituality. Never for one moment allow her to doubt your spiritual sincerity.
YOU'RE NOT THE DOMESTIC TYPE
The doorbell rings just as she is settling down to a nap, and there is no one else in the house to answer it. She opens the door a little reluctantly.

"Oh, it's you, Arthur," she says in relief. "Come in. I thought it might be someone special."

"I'm not interrupting anything, am I?" say, smiling as you enter the living room. Smile nicely; youthfully. "I won't go away, at any rate. Not unless you're very hard and cruel. I worked too hard to get here."

"It's all right," she says, sitting down and patting her hair in back. "I was going to lie down and try to sleep, out of sheer boredom. There's nothing I really have to do. But you should be at work. Why aren't you?"

"I didn't feel like working." Frown and look at her defiantly. "Good Lord, why should a man work all the time? I hate the bloody office anyway, and you know it."

She shakes her head at you, but smiles. "I ought to scold you. But I know too well how you feel."

"Why don't you lie down even if I am here? Go on over to the chaise-longue; I'll tuck your feet up."

"Gracious!" she cries. "You'll have me spoiled if you're too attentive. Bob hasn't your touching respect for my age."

Thump the chair as you bend over to arrange the quilt. "Alice, that isn't funny. It never was funny. At any rate, you mustn't tell Bob how nice I am to you, or his dislike of me will overflow all bounds. That would be a nuisance. I'd have to visit you in the afternoons all the time, and they wouldn't like that at the damned office."

"No, and you wouldn't ever get to see my new dinner dress."

Sit down on the edge of the chair. "And I'd have to stay away on weekends; I'd have to start playing golf, and I hate it. It's much nicer to come here and talk."

She laughs. "Yes, I know you think so. You'd rather talk than do anything else, wouldn't you?"

"Wouldn't you?" you counter. "But this sub rosa arrangement might have its advantages. If I had to be furtive you might be forced to take me seriously."

"You're a silly little boy," she says, looking worried.

"Of course I am. I only wish you said it oftener. If you would only promise me to say every morning and every evening 'What a silly boy Arthur is,' I'd feel better about going home so often."

"It wouldn't be a difficult promise to make," she says thoughtfully. "Perhaps I do it anyway. You're awfully silly sometimes."

"Good! At any rate, that would mean that you would say my name twice a day."

"Heavens!"

"It did sound sentimental, didn't it? Well, forget it. You know, I am serious about Bob: I wish he'd dislike me a little more actively."

She sits up and speaks with decision. "Arthur! You know well enough that Bob doesn't dislike you at all."

"Is that it?" you ask, sorrowfully. "Then it's his maddening indifference that I can't forgive him. I won't forgive him, anyway, so you might as well give up."

"If it would make you feel any better, he said just the other evening, 'Why doesn't that kid get to work? He's been hanging around here a lot longer than he would if I were his father.'"

"Yes," you answer, "that helps. That helps. I feel almost kindly toward him now. I'm glad you told me."

"You know well enough you like Bob!"

Shake your head. "It's just another of my worries. I do like Bob. I love Bob. He's such a child."

She giggles. "Well, I wish he could hear you."

"Yes, isn't it funny? We go around feeling paternal about each other and you lie there and laugh at both of us. Let's not talk about him any more. I'm not a sub rosa visitor yet; I haven't any right to talk. Where's Betty?"

4. YOU'RE NOT THE DOMESTIC TYPE

"I sent her out to the Park for the afternoon." She looks out of the window. "We've had such wretched weather until today. She'll be heartbroken when she finds out you were here. Now that the family's all discussed and taken care of, tell me how you are. Have you been doing anything wicked lately? Tell me some gossip about the younger generation."

"What do I know about the younger generation? I haven't been playing around. It's queer restless weather. I've been trying to write. I'm surprised you haven't noticed this air. There's something in it. Even you must have noticed. It isn't exactly wild. Spiritually provocative, I think—whatever that means."

"Why shouldn't I have noticed it?" she asks.

"You!" you cry bitterly. "A sublimely wise person like you? Alice dearest, why should you have noticed it? Or if you did, why should you admit it?"

She raised her eyebrows, somewhat surprised. "You sound angry," is all she says. "What's the matter?"

"Nothing. I'm in a bad temper."

"You really are," she says wonderingly. "I've never seen you like this. Won't you tell me what's the matter?"

"Oh, for God's sake! Why won't you get angry? Why won't you tell me to get out?"

"Arthur, what is the matter?" She speaks gently.

"I wish you'd get angry, just once. I'd like to fight and fight with you. I'd like to make you cry. I could, too, if I only knew how to begin."

She looks at you in silence. Then go on—"Sit up, Alice! Sit up and slap me. Stop looking so damned comfortable. You don't really feel comfortable."

"But I do," she protests. "I'm sorry, but I do." It is funny, but she doesn't laugh.

"No you aren't. You're sure enough of yourself; you're secure, but you don't like all this any more than I do."

"All what?"

"All—all that you don't like. Why can't you tell me? I keep hoping you will, but you never do. Why can't you tell me? I tell you everything. You have every bit of me. You make me tell you everything and then you never give anything back."

"Arthur!" she cries, hurt.

"I can't help it." Lean closer to her startled face. "There's just one thing I really want. Just one. The one thing I'll never get from you."

"What is it, dear?"

"I want you to tell me the truth. To look at me and say, 'Arthur, I don't really like this at all. I hate this house. I hate being smooth and perfect. I hate my mother for what she did to me, making me like this—'"

"Don't!" she cries.

"'And I hate my daughter for what I am making of her. I hate her when she looks like her father—'"

"No! No!"

"'And I want to die when I realize that I am getting more and more like all of them, all the time.' Go on, Alice. Say it."

She shakes her head slowly, and weeps. "I can't."

"Say it!" you repeat. "I—Alice, I made you cry, didn't I? Never mind. Say it."

"No. The one thing you can never———" she cries convulsively.

"What is it, dearest?"

"You said it yourself," she sobs. "The one thing you can never have. I won't. I can't."

"Stop crying, dearest. Please. I can't hear you when you talk like that. Darling, darling, I'm so sorry I made you cry. I'm so glad. Kiss me. You must, darling. It's the only other thing to do. Alice, you know it is. Kiss me. If you won't talk…. We must, dear."

"Yes," she says.

Take her in your arms.

5. I'M BAD

TYPE:
The very young man with all distinguishing characteristics still in extremely early stages.
SUBJECT:
Any nice girl under fifteen years.
APPARATUS:
1 Porch swing.
REMARKS:
This lesson is relegated to the use of the kiddies; it is good for very little else. In this day of experience and the single standard it is passé, and I include it more as a curiosity than anything else. The beginner should know the fundamental principles, at any rate. For older participants in the game who wish to try their luck along these lines, I suggest more restraint. A few dark hints will go farther than any amount of explicit description. The imagination of an innocent girl can work wonders with a very slight encouragement.

I'M BAD

"But it is different," says the little girl, with an eager note in her voice. You give up the argument for a time and sit in silence, hearing only the creaking of the porch swing's chain above the noises of the summer night.

She takes up the conversation again.

"I mean that supposing I should want to do all those things—some girls do, you know—well, I couldn't. Of course it isn't likely I should want to. I don't see any fun in hanging on to the under part of a train——"

"Riding the blinds," you say, patiently.

"All right; riding the blinds. But there might be something. Like—like staying up all night, perhaps, when it isn't New Year's. Bob used to do that. Mother didn't think it was particularly terrible if he just said he was studying, but I can't even do that. It isn't fair. Here I am a senior in high school and practically grown up and they'll always treat me like a baby just because I'm a girl."

"Yeah," say, as she stops for breath, "it's a shame." And this is as far as your sympathy goes. After all there isn't much else to say. Nevertheless she feels slightly resentful.

"You don't have to be so satisfied about it," she says.

"I'm not satisfied. Only I don't know what I'm supposed to do about it. I think myself you girls are pretty darned lucky. A man has to look out for himself, and believe me sometimes it isn't so much fun as you think."

"Well, even if———"

"No, you can say things like that for hours, but you can't really tell until you have to try it. Why, I'd just like to see you in some of those situations."

She is really impressed.

"What situations?"

"Aw, I couldn't tell you. A fellow couldn't really talk about some of it."

"Oh, go on! I wouldn't tell anyone!"

"You bet you wouldn't! What if I told you that I was caught in a Raid?"

"Really? You're not kidding? What kind of a raid?"

"Why, a—a Raid. There's just one kind. The cops come in and pretty soon the music stops and———"

"Where?"

"'Xpect me to tell? Oh, well, then—Place called the Yellow Mill."

"Oo, gee! Were you alone?"

"Was I alone! Don't be such a dumb-bell. Of course I wasn't alone. Do you suppose a fellow goes to those cabarets alone? Why, they wouldn't let him in!"

"Then who was with you?"

"Never you mind. Some other men and some girls."

"What girls? Anyone in school?"

"Maybe and maybe not."

"Honest? Then it was. I'll bet it was Eleanor."

"Well, it just wasn't. What do you think Eleanor is? A man wouldn't take a NICE girl to the Yellow Mill."

"Why—why Walter, you don't know any other kind, do you?"

"Say, don't judge everybody by yourself."

"Well—what happened?"

"I told you what happened. The cops came in and the music stopped and some of the girls sort of screamed and then the cops started looking for booze."

"Did you have any?"

"Well of course we had had some, but by the time———"

"Oh, Walter!"

"Gosh, don't you think a fellow has to have a drink sometimes? By the time they came we had finished it."

"What was it?"

"You wouldn't know the difference if I told you. It was wine. Elmer got it from his old man."

"Elmer Busby?"

"Nevermind. Well———"

5. I'M BAD

"It was!"

"Well, what if it was? Do you want to hear about this?"

"Oh, yes."

"Well, keep quiet. Well, there wasn't any left when the cop came over to us, so he couldn't prove anything. He just looked at us and said 'All right. Outside!'"

"Then what?"

"Why—then we went home."

"Gee, I'd have been scared to death."

"Sure you would. Any girl would have been."

She sighs and looks out over the front lawn.

"Maybe I wouldn't have been scared, though. Maybe——"

"Sure you would have!"

"No, wait a minute. Maybe it would be fun to be scared sometimes."

"Well, I'd think so, myself, but a girl wouldn't. A nice girl."

"Why, Walter! What a thing to say!"

"Well, I mean it. Look at the way all of you act—'Oh, no, it wouldn't be right—do you think we ought to?'"

"What are you talking about?"

"You. That's just what you said the other night after the party when I tried——"

"Well, really, Walter, I don't see what that has to do with raids."

"Well, it's the same thing."

"Just because I didn't let you kiss me?"

"Well, why didn't you?"

"I don't like kissing."

"You just don't care. You never do let me kiss you. You don't know anything about it. That's the way girls are. No wonder you never have any fun."

"Walter, I think you're really bad."

"Sure I'm bad! I have a good time. You don't."

"No, I don't. But I didn't mean that."

"You're afraid. That's all."

"Walter, I guess——" she stops.

"What?"

"I guess you can kiss me once. Don't tell anybody."

Silence.

"There now. What did you think?"

"I didn't like it. It was horrid. If you tell anybody I'll never speak to you again."

"Well, then, try it again. I won't tell anybody. Come on! What do you think I am? Sure I won't tell anybody."

"Oh, Walter, I bet you think I'm terrible." "Of course I don't. Don't be a dumb-bell." A sudden voice calls from the house.

"Willa! Willa, it's ten-thirty!"

"Oh, Walter, I have to go."

"Good night. Whatcha crying about? What is it, Willa?"

"Oh, you just think I'm terrible!"

"Honest I don't. Can I come over tomorrow night?"

"You know you don't want to. Oh, Mother's calling again."

"Sure I want to."

"All right."

"Good night. Listen, Willa. Honest I think it's all right. I think you're a good sport. Honest. Good night."

6. AN UGLY OLD THING LIKE ME

TYPE:
The unscrupulous man without too much pride when it comes to women. Seemingly frank and open; the rough diamond with a soft heart; Punch wanting to be Hamlet.
SUBJECT:
Tender-hearted and impulsive. A very sweet character.
APPARATUS:
1 Automobile
1 Package cigarettes.
REMARKS:
Scarcely a girl in the world is trained to be on her guard against pity. As a rule a young woman is sure that she is a difficult proposition because of her knowledge of the world and its wicked ways. She is looking, not for weakness, but for strength to combat; for presumption so that she may step on it. It does not occur to any normal girl that she might be taken unawares as an angel of consolation.
AN UGLY OLD THING LIKE ME
It is evening, and you are driving home from dinner in the country. It is a warm summer night and too early to be going back; you have already made a remark to that effect. Suddenly you turn the car into a private-looking road that leads away from the stream of home-going cars.

"Now what?" she asks.

"I want to show you a place I found once. Are you in any particular hurry?"

"No. What is this place?"

"You'll find out in a minute.... Here we are." The car comes to a stop in a natural sort of amphitheater, banked by high walls of rock on one side and well enclosed by shrubbery that is just becoming impassable with the full foliage of midsummer.

"It's an old quarry," explain to her. "Nice, isn't it? I suppose in the daytime it's full of picnic people, but I like it."

"So do I," she answers. There is a silence, and you both light cigarettes.

"Quiet," you mutter. In the deep stillness the air seems full of life. Some animal crashes through the bushes, but the moonlight is not so bright as it seemed and you cannot see him. You sigh, throw your cigarette out onto the ground, and take the girl into your arms. She does not resist at first, except to say "Quit! You'll burn yourself." Then she too casts aside her cigarette and settles down comfortably. But you are too urgent for her.

"Wait a minute," she gasps, sitting up with some difficulty and putting a careful hand to her hair. "What's the matter with you?"

"Nothing. I'm only human, that's all."

"Well, you weren't acting human."

"Sorry. Will you forgive me?"

"Sure."

There is another silence, until she has to object again.

"Really," she protests, "I don't know what's the matter with you tonight. You've never acted like this before."

"I'm terribly sorry, really. I couldn't stand it if I thought I'd offended you. We've been good friends; I don't see why I have to spoil it like this."

"Oh, it's all right. I understand."

"You're awfully sweet, do you know it?"

"Am I really?"

"Much sweeter than anybody else."

"Silly!"

"Ann, I do love you."

"Well then, give me another cigarette."

"No, not just now. Please!"

But after a little interlude of quiet, she protests.

"Arthur, listen. You simply must behave. I don't feel that way; can't you see? I like you a lot, but I just don't feel that way. You can't make me feel that way, either. I'm sorry. I'll have to get mad in a minute."

Don't answer, but stare gloomily at the steering-wheel. She is a little worried.

"Arthur, what's the matter? I wish you wouldn't act that way. It makes me feel so mean. I don't want to be mean. I just thought it would be better to tell the truth."

Sigh and pat her hand.

"You're perfectly right, dear. It's just like you—honest even if you're cruel."

"Don't be so silly. It isn't cruel. I can't help it if I can't feel that way. I never feel that way."

"Never?"

"Arthur, you know I like you better than anybody."

6. AN UGLY OLD THING LIKE ME   35

"No, you don't."
"How can you tell? I don't usually lie."
"Nobody likes me."
"Why, Arthur!" She pulls your head over to hers and kisses you. "There, silly."
"Never mind, Ann," say sadly. "Never mind. You don't have to. You can always be perfectly honest with me. I understand."
"Oh, you do not either!" She is impatient. "You don't understand me at all, if you're going to sulk like that. Here, kiss me."
Then bury your face in her neck.
"Oh, Ann, you're so sweet and I'm such a mess. I'm going to take you home. I'll just make a fool of myself."
"Why, Arthur?" she says, gently. "Don't feel so badly. I understand."
"You always understand, dear."
"I can't go home while you feel so badly. I want to be a friend of yours, Arthur."
"Never mind. It's all right. I know all about it. I don't blame you."
"Blame me? For what?"
"For not liking me Like That."
"Like what?"
"Never mind. I should have thought of it before. You're too sweet; you should have told me. Then I wouldn't have bothered you."
"But Arthur, you don't bother me! What do you mean?"
"Please, Ann, I don't want to talk about it."
"You have to, now. You've started. I've got to know. What is it?"
"Never mind. I'm going to take you home."
"You are not! I won't go home. You sit right there and explain yourself."
"Oh, darling, please let me take you home! Of course I understand. I should have thought of it right away. An ugly old thing like me…."
"Oh, Arthur!" She cries out in pain. "Arthur, how could you think of such a thing! Look at me!"
But don't. She turns your face toward hers by gripping your ears. You are crying, and looking at you she begins to cry too, in pity.
"Arthur, how could you? How could you hurt me so?"
Put your arm around her and pat her on the shoulder.
"Never mind, Ann. Never mind, old girl, it's all right."
"Kiss me," she murmurs, from the depths of your coat-collar.
"No."
"Yes. Please, Arthur."
"You don't want to. You don't feel that way. You're just sorry for me."
"No, no, no! Kiss me!"
Kiss her. She clings to your lips in an ecstasy of renunciation.
"Oh, Ann!" cry, with a break in your voice.
"What, darling? Never mind. Kiss me again."

"Ann, you'd better be careful. Really, you'd better be careful."

"Never mind, darling."

"Ann, are you sure you won't be sorry?"

She doesn't answer.

"An ugly old thing like me, Ann...." But as might be expected, she clings to your coat lapel even harder.

"Ah, Ann, loveliest ... you're not just sorry for me?"

Perhaps she shakes her head. You aren't sure.

"Because, Ann," you add, in an uncertain voice from which you try to keep the triumph, "I'm only human."

There is no objection.

7. BE INDEPENDENT!

TYPE:

The young man who can be sincere in declaration of his radical sympathies. Any one who does not really believe in his expressed opinions will probably fail.

SUBJECT:

Passionately impersonal; burning with zeal to destroy the wrongs of the world. Not much given to paying attention to her own emotions, preferring rather to settle universal problems in the mass.

APPARATUS:

1 City

1 Brief case

REMARKS:

Most of ardent advocates of social improvement are the products of conventional environment. They are inclined to class together all of the rules of conduct which they have denounced as part of a deliberate scheme to slow up the progress of humanity's freedom. If you can associate in their minds the conventional concept of morality with the mossgrown ideas of property and government so horrible to the advanced thinker, you are well on the road to success.

BE INDEPENDENT!

Walking home from the meeting of the Social Science Club, you are more quiet than usual. It is strange that you should be quiet at all; you aren't that type. Both of you love to talk; your intimacy has grown up in spite of, rather than because of this tendency. You became acquainted two or three months before, across the crowded room of the Communist Club when you both leaped to your feet to refute some heretical statement by the speaker of the evening, who had expressed an unsound and intolerant view concerning Union rule. You had cried out together in protest, turned and looked at each other, faltered, and sat down. Then you both had risen again, even more precipitately, looked at each other again in a less amiable manner, and started to speak again. The crowd laughed. At last she had bowed to you jerkily and sat down again, leaving the field to you.

But when she heard what you had to say she did not dislike you so much.

You expressed her views exactly. To be sure, you did not say all there was to be said, and when you finished she had to make several additions. But after the meeting you waited for each other and took up the thread of the argument again. You walked five miles that night and didn't notice. Ever since then you have been seeing a good deal of each other, at little Russian restaurants where each pays his own check, at concerts where you each firmly buy your own tickets, and even at her home, where her family gazes upon you with disfavor and tries to persuade her to wear a hat when she goes out with you.

Tonight there is a tension in the air between you, and you do not know what to do about it. She has been quarreling with her family and you have discussed it backwards and forwards and all around; there was no more to say.

"I don't understand you at all," repeat for the twentieth time. "You're so intelligent about everything but your own affairs. Can't you see that you must attack your own problem with an impersonal sort of attitude? It's the only sensible way to do anything."

"Yes, I know," she answers, gloomily, "but you don't understand, exactly. I have to battle against all the fifteen years that I was under their influence, besides fighting them. There's an element within myself that I can't manage. All sorts of feelings——"

"I know," sympathetically, "anachronistic ideas of duty, and filial fondness, and so forth. They work on all that. Thank God my mother deserted me when I was a baby. Father's different."

"You're lucky," she says. "It makes me furious. After all, I'm of age, and a lot more intelligent than they'll ever be…. Well, we've said all that. I'll just have to let it work itself out."

"It won't," you assure her. "The only way to settle a thing of this sort is to cut it all off. Why don't you go away?"

"How can I?" she says. "I haven't the moral courage to hold out against them. I could go down and live with Marya for a week or so, but you know what would happen. First Ellen would walk in and talk to me, pretending to admire me but holding her skirts away from the furniture all the time. She'd tell me that Mother hasn't been well lately, and then they'd invite me to the house for dinner and they'd act simply angelic and rather pitiful, and then I'd come back. I always do; it's happened before. I know I'm weak, but it's stronger than my intelligence."

"Of course that's one thing I'll never be able to understand. How anyone could stand that house for two hours passes my comprehension, and you've been living there all your life. How do you do any work?"

"I don't," she says, simply. "I haven't really done anything definite since the last election. You can't work any conviction into your speeches if there are a lot of materialists around all the time. Oh, I ought to starve! How can I go on pretending like this?"

7. BE INDEPENDENT!   39

"Never mind. You're getting there. There's nothing wrong with a person that could get away from her environment as completely as you have. But I can see that it's a struggle."

"Thank you," she says, gratefully. You walk on in silence.

"Martha," you say at last, "I know one way out."

"What is it?"

"Come with me."

"With you? But where?"

"Come on home with me. I'll tell Father that you're going to stay there, and that'll be all there is to it. He won't object; he knows better."

"Oh, I couldn't," she says, hastily.

"Why not? It would settle things with your family. I know that type. They'd never bother you again; they would cut you off completely."

She is staggered, and obviously does not know how to answer.

"You're a real friend," she says, at last. "It's good of you to offer. But...."

"Not so generous, after all. Certainly I don't have to tell you that I love you and all that, do I? We know better than to waste our time with such sentimental stuff. But you know that I'd be only too glad...."

"I don't know," she says, thoughtfully. "Honestly, I never thought about it. It's part of my training, I suppose, but it's hard to decide to do a thing like that, right away."

"Think of it in a sensible way," you urge. "Try to throw away those inhibitions. You know well enough that in the course of time we would be lovers. Isn't this better than slinking and being furtive about it, and fooling your family? I'd hate it. As a matter of fact, I have been worrying about it. This would be such a fine, brave thing for you to do. Come on, Martha, be independent. Prove to yourself that you're something more than an average female who wants nothing but security."

"But it's so difficult," she says. "You don't understand. It would kill Mother."

"You know it wouldn't. She might think that she's going to die, but she won't. People don't die over such things. And if she did," you add, superbly, "she wouldn't have any right to. No one has any right to die because someone else lives up to her convictions."

"That doesn't help it, somehow," she says.

"Martha, admit to yourself that it's the only thing to do. You can't go on like this. If you do, they'll sell you to some capitalist for a marriage license and a promise that he'll leave you money when he dies. You'll be part of the same vicious circle. You can't play at both of the games, Martha. If you don't take your freedom when you have the chance I'll have to decide that you're insincere."

She looks very undecided and unhappy. "I don't know what's the matter," she confesses, "but I can't."

Stop and take her arm. She turns around and faces you in the dark street. It is very late and quiet.

"Listen, Martha," you say gravely, "it's up to you. I don't want to persuade you to do anything that you don't really feel you want to do. But I think that I understand you. You have a beautiful nature, Martha. You have a splendid mind that your family weren't able to spoil. As soon as you are strong enough to cast off all the deadly conventions that they've tied you with, you'll be able to do real things for the world. And yet that isn't what I want to say to you now. I respect and admire you, Martha, and I want you. You want me. What else is there to this business? Come with me, Martha, and we'll work together. Throw away that background of yours. Step out into the light."

"Oh, Michael!" she cries. Your face relaxes, and you smile.

Say, "There now, let's do it all, right now. Go home and get your things. I'll go with you, if you like. Then they can do what they want to; I know you won't back out."

Arm in arm, you walk down the street.

8. WHAT DO YOU THINK YOUR HUSBAND'S DOING?

TYPE:

The man who likes to use an appeal to reason to gain his ends. He is untrained, but possesses a certain native subtlety.

SUBJECT:

Small and thirty, overworked, with a face that has been prettier, but which could be much less pretty.

APPARATUS:

Excursion boat.

REMARKS:

This is a system which is based on the simplest and most atavistic of human emotions—jealousy. Reflection upon this fact may deter from its use a number of my students who would regard such an easy and impersonal victory as an affront to their pride and self-confidence as first-rate seducers. It is true that the success of the method is much more the result of the subject's internal conflict than of any remarkable attributes on the part of the student. But it is up to the seducer to be there at the psychological moment to suggest action. It takes a large amount of tact and self-control to bring the situation to the point of this suggestion without arousing the suspicions of the subject. It is not too easy. Do not treat it with contempt.

WHAT DO YOU THINK YOUR HUSBAND'S DOING?

It is night on the boat; the last evening of the See-America-First-Cruise; Excursion tickets good until August thirty-first; Send the wife and kiddies if you can't go yourself. It is night and all the children have gone to bed, allowing a blessed quiet to creep from the darkness and shroud the boat in wistful romance. Two figures stand in the bow.

She: Well, home tomorrow.

You: Yes. (Sigh) Back to work.

She: I do hope it'll be cooler. But there, it never does get any cooler until the middle of September or after, so what's the use of hoping? I didn't have any right running away from the house this time of the year.

You: Sure you did. When you first came on the boat I said to myself, "There's a little woman that sure needs a rest."

She: You did! I didn't know I looked that bad. The doctor told me to take a rest, but land, he's always telling me that.

You: No, I don't mean you looked exactly bad; only sort of thin and pale.

She: (Pleased): Thin! Heavens, I didn't know that I ever looked thin. But it isn't any wonder I'm pale. Goodness knows I never get out of the house.

You: You know, that's one thing I just can't understand about men. The way they let their wives stay at home. Believe me, if I ever get married my wife is going to have the best of everything. And plenty of time to enjoy it, too.

She: Well, I certainly think your wife'll be lucky. But you'll probably have to wait a long time to be earning enough. I guess HE doesn't have it any too easy himself, working all day in an office. Sometimes he comes home mighty tired.

You: Maybe, but don't you believe he has it any near as bad as you do. I'll never forget my poor old mother slaving day in and day out. You know what they say—"Man's work is from sun to sun; it's woman's whole existence" or something like that. I tell you, I grew up to respect women, I did.

(There is a pause while you think about it.)

She (sighing): Well, I certainly like to hear a man talk like that sometimes. I just wish Joe could hear you.

You: Oh, he'd say I didn't know anything about it, seeing as I'm not married.

She: I don't know. Joe's awful reasonable. It was because of him I took this trip. He saw the ad in the paper and he says "Mary, that'd be mighty good for you," he says. And I says, "Yes, but how would you get along?" He says, "Oh, I'll manage." And now I know that when I look at that kitchen I'll just sit down and cry. I do like a nice clean kitchen. He didn't even want me to take the children.

You: Oh well, it's no more than he ought to do. You're a mighty nice little woman; I bet he ought to know it.

She: Aw!

You: I bet he don't know how lucky he is. Married fellows never do. How long have you been married anyway?

She: That's a personal question.

You: Is it? I'm sorry.

She: Don't be silly. I've been married six years.

You: Gee, he must've married you out of high school.

She: Kidder! (She is pleased.) Well, I guess I did get married kind of young.

You: I'll say you did.

She: I think it's better that way, don't you? Keeps kids out of mischief.

You: I don't know. I almost got married, but—I always thought maybe I'd better see the world first.

She: Maybe the Right One didn't come along for you.

You: I guess that was it. Just my luck to find her when—oh, well.

She: What were you going to say?

You: Wouldn't it be too bad if she did come along and I was too late?

She: That's always the way, I guess.

You: Yes, that's always the way.

(Another silence.)

She: You're awful romantic, aren't you? I'd know right away you wasn't a married man.

You: That's funny. It's just what I would have said about you.

She: You could tell right away I was married?

You: No, just the other way around. I said, "Well, here she is!"

She: Here who is?

You: And then I saw your wedding-ring.

She: You know I have a girl friend who always takes off her ring when she goes to a matinee. Joe says to me, "Mary if ever a wife of mine did that I'd give her a good hiding."

You: Yeah? Honest, you'd be surprised at the number of married women there are that lead a fellow on.

She: Really?

You: You bet. You wouldn't know any like that, of course; but the way they act there ought to be a law against it.

She: I always say if a woman isn't happy with her husband she ought to come right out and say so and get divorced or else not show anybody the way she feels.

You: That's the right way to look at it. Of course I guess men don't make it too easy for you either. Now me, whenever I'm tempted I just think of my old mother.

She: It depends on the mother too.

You: Sure.

(A comfortable and agreeing silence, while the boat glides on through the darkness.)

You: It sure is nice to meet a woman who can talk about these things without any—any foolishness. Oh well. Tomorrow it'll all be over.

She: Tomorrow.

(Sigh again and pat her hand on the rail, leaving your hand over hers when the patting is finished.)

You: Don't you think people ought to be broadminded about some things?

She: I guess so. What things?

You: Oh, different things.

She: Sure.
(Emboldened, you put your arm around her. She starts away.)
She: No, don't.
You: Why?
She: It's wrong. You ought to be ashamed.
You: What's wrong about it? We want to, don't we?
She: Say, Joe would kill you if he could hear you.
You: He can't hear me. Aw, be sensible.
She: I'm being sensible. You're a nice fellow; now quit. I'm going in.
You: No, wait a minute. Just a minute. You've got me all wrong. We've been good friends, haven't we?
She: Yes, we have. I didn't know you were going to be like this.
You: Didn't you?
She (blazing): No, I didn't! And what's more——
You: Now, don't get mad. Don't get mad.
She: What's more, Joe would kill you! I told you he'd kill you.
You: There can't be any harm in me putting my arm around you.
She: Sh-h-h!
(The captain passes them in the darkness, muttering "Nice evening, folks." She is frightened, and as you put your arm around her again she does not object.)
You: What harm could there be in it?
She: I wish you'd——
You: Come on, put your face up.
(Kiss her.)
She (bursting into tears): I tell you Joe would kill you.
You: Say, kid, what makes you so sure?
She: What do you mean?
You: What do you think he's doing while you're away?
She: Joe? Why—why——
You: Oh, be sensible. What did he send you away for? What do you think men are anyway?
She (frightened): You're wrong; you don't know Joe.
You: Now listen. You know how easy it is to act this way.
She: No—I won't listen to you.
You: I don't guess he's any different from the rest of us. You been married six years? Say! Don't be dumb. Listen; didn't that schoolmarm in your cabin get off today?
She: No, no.
You: Yes she did. I'm coming around to say good night.
She: But I don't want you to.
You: I don't think you know what you do want.
She: No, I'm going in.
You: We've got a lot to talk about.

She (uncertainly): I oughtn't.
You: What's wrong with it? Don't be dumb.
She: Goodnight. I guess we better say goodbye too.
You: Not yet. Oh, have a little sense, will you? He don't know any more about you than you know about him.
She: Stop talking like that.
You: Well, how about it?
She: Well——
You: Aw, go on.
She: Well——
You: This door locks, don't it?

9. MUSIC GETS ME

TYPE:
The young man with some understanding of music and its effect on the untrained ear.
SUBJECT:
A home girl with no particular leaning toward anything but marriage.
APPARATUS:
1 Victrola
Records as follows:
Venetian Moon
Tea for Two
Merry Widow Waltz
Livery Stable Blues
Peggy O'Neill
Floradora Medley
Valse Bluette
At Dawning
Leibestraum
L'Apres-Midi D'un Faun
Fire Song
Song of India
REMARKS:
The selection of music to be used for seduction is not an arbitrary matter. A different combination is necessary for every variation in temperament. Some day it is to be hoped that the difficulty will be overcome; perhaps someone will be able to compile a catalogue of effective combinations. Until then the student can do no better than his unassisted best.
MUSIC GETS ME
"Wouldn't you think," she says, "we'd have something from last year, anyway? There isn't anything as dead as an old dance record. We used to have parties and break the old ones, I remember. And I made up my mind not to buy any more except Red Seals, because the other ones were out of date in a week. I believe that for a while I spent my whole allowance on records, every month."

"Yes, it's funny how fast they change," you say, balancing a particularly warped disk on your forefinger. "Remember when jazz first came in—all horns and those sweet-potato things? They were awfully loud. Dad said the world was going crazy. And then the toddle."

"Oh yes!" she cries, standing on one foot and bobbing up and down. "It was hard to break the habit when it went out. What are you going to play?"

You wind up the handle, and it squeaks in protest. "Never mind. See if you recognize it."

"Oh, Venetian Moon! That reminds me of something. Do songs mean things to you? Do certain tunes bring back certain thoughts and feelings to you?"

"Sure, whenever I hear Poor Butterfly I think of Lorna Doone. I can't trace the connection exactly, but I always do."

"It must have been played somewhere when you read it," she says. The record is finished, and the needle scrapes with a harsh sound. "It's all rusty," she adds. "I'm going to have it fixed up. I'm tired of the radio anyway. I'd rather choose what I want to hear."

"Here's Tea for Two. That was a pretty good one."

"Yes," she sighs. "I was kissed for the first time when that was being played. What a fearfully old record!"

Wind up the machine again and put it on, then hold out your arms. "Let's dance."

She glides to you. After the first few bars kiss her lightly. She stops, pushing you away. "What's the idea?" she demands.

"I was just trying to revive old memories," you explain. "Come on and finish; I'll be good. Say, you're a peach of a dancer."

"Thanks," she says, going back to the Victrola. "Whose old memories were you reviving then?"

"Oh, don't be funny," you grumble. "Here's a real old-timer." Hold it up for her to read; it is the Merry Widow Waltz.

"Mother used to dance to that," she says. "Let's try to dance in the way they did in the play last year." But you can not imitate the graceful swooping circles of the Viennese. "It's not so good," she decides. "What else is here?"

"Here's something called the Livery Stable Blues. Do you know it? I don't." You put it on, and a dreadful yowling fills the air. She covers her ears.

"Stop it!" she cries. "Take it off! Imagine dancing to that."

"Oh gosh! Here's Peggy O'Neill! That has plenty of memories for me, all right. She turned me down the same evening."

"I'm so sorry, but you were too young to be getting married anyway. Look at this? I wonder why no one ever broke it. I think they played it at my first Prom. It's queer, but the only people I remember at parties are perfectly irrelevant ones; people I just have one dance with, or something. This is having a very bad effect on me. I feel so old and regretful." She sighs and looks in the mirror hanging on the wall.

9. MUSIC GETS ME

"Well then," say, winding up the machine again, "Listen to this and have a real good cry. You weren't born yet when they were playing it." Start to sing with the music. "Oh, tell me, pretty maiden, are there any more at home like you? There are a few—kind sir———"

"I never even heard it," she says. "It's quite catchy, too. They had a lot of good songs, in their way. What are you doing? You'll get all dusty."

You are struggling with a large pile of Red Seals. "Sometimes they have a waltz or something that you can use in these highbrow things," shuffling them. "Here's something; Valse Bluette. It might be good; let's try to dance to it."

But the rhythm is too varied for you. You struggle for a while, and then she breaks away, laughing and breathless.

"No good," she says. "But here's one of my favorites. Do you mind? Wait a minute."

John McCormick's voice rings out richly, marred only by a periodic scratch.

"When-n-n the dawwwn
Flames innnn the skyeeeeee
I—uh—love—uh youuuuuu:
Whennnn the birrrrdlings wake and cryeeeee
I—uh—love—uh yououuuuooooo."

"Isn't that lovely?" she says, raptly. "I always loved that song. Music always GETS me somehow. Let's play it again."

"Wait a minute," you say. "I have something else." The sweet strains of Liebestraum make the air sticky, and her ready laughter is stilled in reverence.

Say, "I don't know if you'll like this one or not. It's a long one."

She sits down on the divan. "Sure. Go ahead. What is it? I don't remember any of them."

"L'Apres-Midi D'Un Faun."

"What?"

"L'Apres-Midi D'Un Faun. It's French. Listen!"

She shakes her head briskly as you turn the record over, and starts to talk. Motion to her to be quiet, and play the second part. She speaks drowsily.

"It's very queer. It's made me sleepy. Are you playing it again? For heaven's sake, why?"

"Well," you explain, "it always sounds better the second time."

Listen to it again, with your hands clasped together. Lean over to her. "It's a funny thing about that music. It gets me." Kiss her.

"I know," she says. "If I listened to it very long I wouldn't be responsible."

"Responsible for what?"

"Oh, just responsible." Kiss her again. She stands up. "Let's play something loud and get waked up."

"This ought to be loud. The Fire Song."

"No," she decides, after a few bars, "it isn't loud enough. I can't wake up. Play the Hymn to the Sun."

"It scratches," you object. "Here's one something like it."

Play the Song of India. She sighs and relaxes.

"I love that," she says, dreamily. "What's that you're going to play?"

Without answering her, put on L'Apres-Midi D'Un Faun.

10. EVERYBODY DOES

TYPE:
Unscrupulous and determined, but subtle.
SUBJECT:
One who is not sure of herself; who hides an inner shrinking by a brave show of sophistication. In her heart is a horrible doubt bred by the reticence of her elders. She is beginning to feel that there are ancient, eternal fibs rife in the cosmos. She is convinced that everyone is in a conspiracy to keep her in ignorance.
APPARATUS:
1 Living room with sofa.
REMARKS:
The young man in our illustration has compunctions about taking advantage of sentiments so like his own, but sheer inertia carries him along. So it will probably be in your case.
EVERYBODY DOES

"I think you're perfectly TERRIBLE," says the girl, smiling as if she doesn't expect to be believed. "Whoever told you all about everything? I wouldn't want to live if I felt that way. Why, what would we be here for?"

"I don't see why we have to be here for anything, particularly," you answer. "What are mosquitoes for?"

She hesitates for only a second.

"So we won't get too lazy. They probably wonder why we're here, slapping them just when they want to eat."

Look through the window to the lawn outside, covered with snow.

"That's an unusual remark for a girl of your sort to make," you muse. "Well, you probably talk that way because this is winter. Now, if I had asked you in July, when there would be plenty of mosquitoes——"

"What ARE you talking about?" she asks. "What do you mean, a girl of my type?"

Laugh and glance at her obliquely. She is very pretty, you think, with that maddeningly serene face of hers. Just now, though she is interested, her expression isn't really with you. You want to do something about it.

"I mean a girl of your type," repeat firmly. "A girl who believes everything she's taught."

She frowns a little.

"Wouldn't it be silly to go to school for as long as I have if I didn't use what they told me?"

"That isn't what school is for," you answer hastily. Lord, what a dumbbell! Why am I here, anyway? But she is pretty.

"You're pretty, anyway," you say aloud.

"But that's awfully mean! Pretty anyway! What do you mean? Don't you think a girl can be pretty and have brains too?"

"Well—brains of a sort." Now what am I in for? "Sure I guess you have brains. I bet you're practical in business things."

"Heavens, no!" she protests. "I can't do a thing. But I was good at school. I was terribly good in Latin."

Turn a little on the sofa and smile at her, leaning back. "Ever have any philosophy courses?"

"Of course," she says promptly. "Three hours a week."

"And Chapel every morning?"

"Every morning."

"What did you do in Philosophy? I know about the Chapel."

"Oh, we studied what all those old birds thought about the world and the mind and reality and those things. And at examinations they asked us to summarize the different points of view."

"And you had Chapel every day?" you persist. This is something.

"I told you. It was compulsory."

"They told you what to think, in Chapel?"

"Oh, no!" she cries. "No. Sometimes the Doctor would talk about smoking for girls, and sometimes about movies. And there is a beautiful sermon that he always gives at Easter, about bread and hyacinths. That's about Art, you know."

Nod thoughtfully. "Yes. He likes Art, doesn't he?"

"You're teasing me," she says, sadly. "Whenever I talk about religion you get that way. I don't see why we're always fighting."

"We're not always fighting, are we? All right, let's stop talking about school. But I did want to ask you something. Why do you think it's so shocking when I say that God isn't watching everything you do?" And you think with some anger at yourself that here you are again.

"I didn't think it was shocking," she says eagerly. "I'm never shocked. I was just surprised when you told Lilian you didn't think He was personal enough to have opinions on Prohibition."

"What makes you think He is?" you ask. Put your arm around her shoulders; she snuggles down comfortably.

"Well," she begins reasonably, "how would we all be here? Don't you think we must have come from—I mean, don't you see that we must be something

10. EVERYBODY DOES 53

like Him? Not so perfect or so big and powerful, but—why everybody knows that!"

"So that makes it all right," you tease her. "If everybody thinks so."

"Well, I guess they've always thought so, for years. And it seems to work. Here we are, aren't we? Don't you think we're improving? It must be right."

"How did we get started on all this, anyway?" You are bored. "It was talking about Prohibition. It always happens."

"Yes, that's how it happened. You fired up when Lilian said it was a success. I'm glad Mother wasn't there to hear you. She's a little afraid of you anyway."

"Is she? Why? I'm safe enough. We just talk—and talk—and talk!" Confound old women!

"I know," she says happily. "I love to talk seriously. We used to have lots of arguments in my room at school, after hours.... No, I think you're right; I don't think Prohibition's a success at all. I think anybody with sense would know it. Look at the way perfectly nice boys get drunk at every party. I almost died the first time my escort did. Dad said he'd shoot the young puppy. Mother says that never used to happen. I think Prohibition is terrible."

"You are pretty," say irrelevantly, and kiss her. She returns the kiss placidly.

"You shouldn't," she says, lazily.

"Why? Don't you like it?"

"Of course not. What made you think I did?"

"Well, most girls do. In fact, I might say that everybody does."

"Not girls!" she protests, shocked.

"For Pete's sake!" you cry, exasperated. "Who on earth told you that? You don't really think so, do you?"

"Why not? Don't you take a lot for granted?"

"I never take anything for granted. Why do you wear blue? Because it's becoming. Well, why do you want to look pretty? So that I'll kiss you. Of course!"

"Don't do that. I don't want you to."

"If I thought you meant it I'd stop. Look here——" Oh Lord, can't I quit it? "Listen. You're not consistent."

"How?"

"You say that whatever people do must be all right, don't you?"

"If everybody does it and it works out."

"Well, doesn't everybody do this?"

"Oh, no!"

"Don't be an idiot! How do you suppose you were born?"

"But my parents were married."

You tear your hair. How can one be reasonable with such stupidity?

"That hasn't any physiological significance!"

"I don't——"

"You COULD have been born without their being married, couldn't you?"

She considers, then smiles triumphantly. "Not with my parents!"

"But what the hell did you and your friends talk about at school?"

"Well, some of the girls might have been fast. They wouldn't say, of course."

"A lot more than you suspected were probably 'fast.'"

She resents this. "I'm not so dumb as you think."

You feel guilty, and at the same time stubborn. You know this feeling: you have had it before and it always gets you into trouble.

"All right. Suppose I talked a little about your friend Lilian? How long have you known her?"

"All my life. Why——" in quick alarm—"do you mean to say that you know anything about Lilian that I don't?"

"I don't want to talk about Lilian. But you're very trusting for your age. Everyone lies to everybody; didn't you know that? Kiss me and forget about it."

"I can't. You have to tell me. Tell me!"

For a moment you feel sorry. You shouldn't have done it; you know it. Your arm tightens about her. You have to stop her somehow; she is going to cry.

"Please don't worry so. Everybody does. Please don't cry, baby. You are a baby. It really doesn't matter, I tell you. Not if everybody does."

"No!"

"All right! I didn't mean it!"

She wipes her eyes and sits up, looking at you curiously.

"Really? Did you mean it? Everybody? Lilian? You?"

"I don't want to talk." You feel miserable. You feel like worrying her some more. Put your arms around her, give her a little shake.

"Stop talking about it!" Kiss her hard; she kisses you with a new quality in her response. There is something defiant in her kiss.

Later, going home, you begin to feel badly again.

"I wish I could control myself. I always get into trouble. That was queer, though. Oh, well."

Pause at the edge of the pavement, watching the sweep of the traffic, "She is pretty."

11. THIS BUSINESS

TYPE:
Any working man who does not have to work too hard to keep his mind on more important matters. An opportunist.
SUBJECT:
A girl of corresponding economic position, preferably a stranger.
APPARATUS:
1 Barber Chair with Accessories.
REMARKS:
The directness of this method calls for a good deal of self-confidence. Delicate or timid personalities should avoid it.
THIS BUSINESS
It is peaceful everywhere in town, but the barber shop is the most peaceful place of all. Two of the boys are working; talking in low tones to their customers; and the third is drowsing in the corner, behind the two-foot square bootblacking establishment. He has long since read all the ancient Libertys and Colliers and newspapers that are lying on the chairs. The air is full of gentle boredom.

Then through the door comes a stranger. She looks about the shop hesitantly; the two men that are sprawled out having haircuts glance at her apathetically through the mirror. Not you, however. You leap to position behind your chair and wave your towel encouragingly, almost lovingly. You feel actually affectionate; it has been a very dull afternoon. She isn't bad either; clean and pink-looking.

"Yes ma'am," you murmur, as you tuck the fragrant towel into the collar of her dress. "Shingle?"

"Not too short, please," she answers. "Just a trim."

Set to work with a flourish. The barber on the end winks at you, but pretend not to see it. All is quiet for a few minutes except for the snipping of the scissors, and then the coon who belongs to the bootblacking establishment shuffles through the door and puts a record on the Victrola in the corner.

Hum the tune and step lively as you reach for the clippers. Catch the customer's eye in the mirror and smile. She responds slightly.

"It may be old," say jovially, "but it's still good."

"I always did like it," she admits.

Bend over and snip critically at a tuft of hair just behind her ear.

"What I say is," murmur confidingly, "I'd rather have a good old tune if it's really good than a lot of new junk. It's funny about songs. I play the clarinet myself. Sometimes you'll have a lot of swell ones and then a year'll go by and you won't have anything worth playing."

"Yes, that's true," says the lady.

"Weren't you in here about a month back?" Pause with upraised scissors to regard your work in the mirror.

"No," she says, "I'm new in town. I was through here once when I was a baby, that's all."

"That's funny. I thought sure I cut your hair once before."

"No, you couldn't have."

"Who did cut it last time?"

"I don't know. A fellow in Dodge City."

"It looks like a Dodge City haircut. They must learn how to cut hair by correspondence in that town." Chuckle at the joke. She is annoyed.

"It looked all right to me," she says promptly.

"Sure," answer her, "it looks all right. I'm not saying it didn't look all right. It's when it gets long the unevenness shows up, but you don't need to worry. It looks all right now."

Work industriously for a minute, then step back again to survey the effect. "Do you want it any shorter on the side there?"

"Whatever you think looks best. I guess you know more about how it ought to look."

"Oh, I wouldn't say that," you protest.

"Sure you do," she says.

"You going to stay in town long?" Select a pair of clippers.

"Yes, I'm here for good, I guess. I've got a job here."

"That's swell," heartily. "We need new people here. Don't we, Jim?"

The second barber jumps and looks up. "Eh?" he says.

"I was just telling the little lady we need new people here."

"Oh, uh, yes. Sure."

"Yes," you resume, "it's a good town, but sometimes you get to wishing there were more people. You know, young people."

"Yes, I must say it doesn't look very lively to me," she says. "Of course I'm used to Dodge City; that's pretty lively."

"Well now, I don't know. You have to make your own excitement, of course. But it ain't so bad. If you get in with the right kind, of course. A place like this, it's pretty important what kind you get in with."

One by one, the other customers leave and their barbers drift outside to loaf in the sun. Tiny grains of powder dance in the beams that slant to the floor of the shop.

"Do you mind the clippers?"

11. THIS BUSINESS

"No, go ahead."

Work a minute in silence.

"Say," you begin, "would you mind my asking you a personal question?"

"It depends on what it is." She lowers her eyes to her lap.

"Are you married?"

She smiles. "You've got a nerve. No, I ain't."

"That's good."

"Why? It's none of your business, is it?"

"You don't act very friendly, do you?"

"Well, I don't believe in acting as friendly as some people do."

Laugh heartily and start to comb her hair tightly over her forehead.

"You know, you got pretty hair," you say. She glances at it rather complacently in the mirror, and tips her head. Resume impulsively, "You know, this business is awfully hard on a man of my calibre."

She is unsympathetic. "What do you want me to do about it?"

"Nothing. I was just wondering if you were busy tonight."

She giggles. "Who wants to know?"

"Ah, cut that out!" you cry, flicking the big duster on her neck. "I want to know. Who did you think?"

"I don't know about tonight," she muses.

"I've got a flivver. There ought to be a dance somewhere. I bet you're a mighty good little dancer."

"I'd like to," she admits, "but I don't think I'd better."

"Why not?"

"Well, I'm just starting out in this place. You know how it is."

"What's the harm? A ride and a little drink won't hurt you. If you like I'll ask a couple of friends. Listen...."

One of the other barbers comes in again, and you stop abruptly. The haircut is obviously finished. Untuck the towel with lingering fingers and step to the door with her as she fumbles in her purse.

"Fifty cents, ma'am," you say loudly, and add in a low voice, "Listen. Eight o'clock, see? What address?"

"Four eighty-three Garden. But I don't know...."

"Oh, who'll ever know about it? Eight o'clock, O.K. Fifty cents, seventy-five, one dollar. Thank you ma'am."

"Say Jim, did you see that!"

12. GAME LITTLE KID

TYPE:
The out-of-door man who smokes a pipe and can hit twice in the same place when chopping wood. One who believes in Pure Womanhood; who would die for his country and kill any man with designs on his wife.
SUBJECT:
Rather young, wistful and easy to flatter. Does not know what she believes, but reflects the philosophy of any companion.
APPARATUS:
1 Picnic Spot
1 Fire
1 Pipe
REMARKS:
They make very attractive flannel shirts nowadays.
GAME LITTLE KID
She watches you lazily while you souse the dishes in the lake and wipe them clumsily. She feels rather guilty about it, but at the beginning of the hike you have insisted on taking care of everything. It is your party. And it is a nice party, too. The moon is there, and the air is warm, and somewhere there is a flower that smells very sweet. She closes her eyes and leans against the rock and feels happy.

Knock the ashes out of your pipe and sit down by her, taking her hand in yours. "Swell night," you say.

"Oh, yes! I'm having a good time."

"So am I. I've had a better time today than I can remember since I don't know when."

"Really?" she protests smiling. "How about that race at Mackinac?"

"That was pretty good too. Only you weren't along. It could have been perfect."

She laughs easily. "I'd have been in the way. You've never tried telling me anything else before. What's the matter with you tonight? Getting soft?"

"Not much use of that, is there?" You both chuckle. "You're too cagey. I couldn't say anything nice to you even if I meant it. You'd bite my head off."

"Sure!"

Push her in mock exasperation, then take her hand again. She is a little uneasy about it, and leans over to tie her boot-lace more securely.

"Well, it's all right with me," say suddenly. "You know, you're a pretty game kid."

"Oh, I don't know. I don't think so."

"You sure are. Lots of people must have told you so before. I like you. Do you know it?"

"Glad you do," she says. "I like you."

"There, that's just what I mean." Fill your pipe again. "Saying it out, frankly, like that."

"Why shouldn't I, if it's true?"

"Well, I don't really know why you shouldn't. But most girls wouldn't. You know how women are."

"Sure," she says, largely.

"Gee," you cry. "The way you say that! Funny kid."

"Now, what sounded funny about that?"

"Oh, I don't know. It sounded so boyish. You're just like a boy, now that I think of it." Turn and smile at her.

"Thanks! I always wanted to be a boy."

"I'll bet you did. Gosh, though, I wouldn't if I were you."

"Why not?"

"Girls have a much better time. I wouldn't mind if someone had to buy my tickets and take me out to dinner once in a while."

She thinks about it for a minute, poking the fire with the toe of her heavy boot. "I'm not sure," she says slowly. "We pay for it, in a way. Suppose you had to see as much of some of the idiots that we do? You can just ask anyone you want; we have to wait till we're asked."

"Yes, that's so. Some of them are pretty bad, I guess." You laugh. "Anyway, I always thought some of your friends were, but I never dared to say so. What's the matter with 'em, exactly?"

"They're so stupid!" she cries. "They think all a girl is good for is to paw. They haven't any idea of real fun at all."

"I know." Pat her arm comfortingly. "Just grab you as soon they look at you, don't they? Most men are like that, I guess. I don't understand it myself. I'm no saint, but I couldn't have anything to do with a girl unless I liked her. Do you understand?"

"Of course," she says, flushing a little in excitement. "I feel that way exactly. I'm so glad you do too. I was beginning to think that men were just different. Most of them——"

"Sure. Honestly, do they bother you so much?" You frown.

"Yes, even me. Can you imagine? Me!"

"That just shows you. If you'll pardon my being frank…."

"Of course."

"I can't imagine anything like that, with you."

12. GAME LITTLE KID

"Certainly. I know. That's why we get along so well, isn't it?"

"We are—friends, aren't we?"

"Sure!"

Squeeze her hand and puff at your pipe, thinking deeply. Then sigh, and say, "Funny thing, sex."

"Isn't it!"

"You know, it's wonderful to be able to talk like this to a girl. I couldn't if you were really a—a woman in my mind. But I don't feel that way about you at all. You're my friend. You don't appeal to me that way."

She wonders vaguely if she likes that. But she answers quickly. "Thank you. I know you mean it. You know, a friendship like that is valuable to me, too. I need it. I used to think that no matter how much I tried, it was just impossible to have a man for a real friend."

"Really? Then we're square, because you mean a lot to me."

Put your arm around her and look into the fire.

"That's another thing," she says, thoughtfully. "That's another reason I wish I could be a man. You have an awfully easy time with that sort of thing, don't you?"

"What? Gosh, no. I don't see how anybody could think so."

"Really? I always thought you did. I don't know very much about it, but——"

"I'm glad you don't!" you growl with such fervor that she is surprised.

"What's the matter? You shouldn't care anything about what I do—like that. Not if we're friends the way you say."

"Well, I'll tell you." Pull her closer to your shoulder. "I can't break away from a funny idea I have about you. I want you to stay just as straight as you are. It's a queer thing, sex. I don't want you spoiled. That fine straightness of yours is so rare. I guess I'm selfish to want anyone to live up to my ideals, but I do want you to keep it." Give her a little hug.

She answers gravely. "Yes, I know. I want to stay the way I am, too. I don't know how I really feel about it, I guess, but I do—I mean, I like myself now, do you see? It's awfully hard to express."

"I know. Gee, you're a peach, kid. I do like you."

"Thanks...." Kiss her softly on the cheek. "Look!" she cries, sitting up a little straighter. "There's a shooting star."

"It's awfully nice. Come back here. Afraid of me?"

"Of course not!" But she sits up.

"You don't trust me?"

"Don't! Of course I do."

"Then why act like that? You'll hurt my feelings."

"Oh, I didn't mean to!" She settles back against your shoulder. Kiss her on the mouth; she struggles away.

"What's the matter, dear?" you murmur. "I thought you trusted me. What's the matter?"

"Why, I didn't mean—I do trust you. Only...." She stops and looks away from you.

"Then what is it? I don't understand. Do you mean you—you can't trust yourself? I thought you were so sensible about these things."

"Of course I can. I'm not a man!"

"No, dear. But you're a woman, aren't you? Are you afraid, really?"

"I'm not afraid. I just didn't want to."

"Oh, I'm sorry...."

"I didn't mean I didn't want to."

"Just don't care?"

"Not exactly that...."

Laugh. "You're a darling. I'm going to kiss you again. That'll be all right?"

"Sure, I guess so."

"You really liked it."

"A little."

"Don't keep moving away like that! I'll think you hate me. You just said we were friends."

"Yes, but...."

"Comfortable?"

"Yes, but...."

"There now, I won't bother you any more if you'll only show that you trust me. Darling!"

The fire smolders, unnoticed.

12. GAME LITTLE KID

"Certainly. I know. That's why we get along so well, isn't it?"

"We are—friends, aren't we?"

"Sure!"

Squeeze her hand and puff at your pipe, thinking deeply. Then sigh, and say, "Funny thing, sex."

"Isn't it!"

"You know, it's wonderful to be able to talk like this to a girl. I couldn't if you were really a—a woman in my mind. But I don't feel that way about you at all. You're my friend. You don't appeal to me that way."

She wonders vaguely if she likes that. But she answers quickly. "Thank you. I know you mean it. You know, a friendship like that is valuable to me, too. I need it. I used to think that no matter how much I tried, it was just impossible to have a man for a real friend."

"Really? Then we're square, because you mean a lot to me."

Put your arm around her and look into the fire.

"That's another thing," she says, thoughtfully. "That's another reason I wish I could be a man. You have an awfully easy time with that sort of thing, don't you?"

"What? Gosh, no. I don't see how anybody could think so."

"Really? I always thought you did. I don't know very much about it, but——"

"I'm glad you don't!" you growl with such fervor that she is surprised.

"What's the matter? You shouldn't care anything about what I do—like that. Not if we're friends the way you say."

"Well, I'll tell you." Pull her closer to your shoulder. "I can't break away from a funny idea I have about you. I want you to stay just as straight as you are. It's a queer thing, sex. I don't want you spoiled. That fine straightness of yours is so rare. I guess I'm selfish to want anyone to live up to my ideals, but I do want you to keep it." Give her a little hug.

She answers gravely. "Yes, I know. I want to stay the way I am, too. I don't know how I really feel about it, I guess, but I do—I mean, I like myself now, do you see? It's awfully hard to express."

"I know. Gee, you're a peach, kid. I do like you."

"Thanks...." Kiss her softly on the cheek. "Look!" she cries, sitting up a little straighter. "There's a shooting star."

"It's awfully nice. Come back here. Afraid of me?"

"Of course not!" But she sits up.

"You don't trust me?"

"Don't! Of course I do."

"Then why act like that? You'll hurt my feelings."

"Oh, I didn't mean to!" She settles back against your shoulder. Kiss her on the mouth; she struggles away.

"What's the matter, dear?" you murmur. "I thought you trusted me. What's the matter?"

"Why, I didn't mean—I do trust you. Only...." She stops and looks away from you.

"Then what is it? I don't understand. Do you mean you—you can't trust yourself? I thought you were so sensible about these things."

"Of course I can. I'm not a man!"

"No, dear. But you're a woman, aren't you? Are you afraid, really?"

"I'm not afraid. I just didn't want to."

"Oh, I'm sorry...."

"I didn't mean I didn't want to."

"Just don't care?"

"Not exactly that...."

Laugh. "You're a darling. I'm going to kiss you again. That'll be all right?"

"Sure, I guess so."

"You really liked it."

"A little."

"Don't keep moving away like that! I'll think you hate me. You just said we were friends."

"Yes, but...."

"Comfortable?"

"Yes, but...."

"There now, I won't bother you any more if you'll only show that you trust me. Darling!"

The fire smolders, unnoticed.

13. PROMISE ME YOU WON'T

TYPE:

Large, clumsy, good-hearted. A shrewd business man, whatever that means. Usually married.

SUBJECT:

Intelligent, pretty little specimen of Independent Womanhood, just beginning to question the desirability of a lifetime among the file cases.

APPARATUS:

1 Small Apartment

2 Chairs

1 Batik Drapery

2 Bed-Sofas

1 Japanese Print

1 Indifferently Good Caricature in Crayon.

REMARKS:

Somehow the sight of a man being paternal arouses in woman a protective instinct on her own part; an indulgent affection compounded of amusement and gratitude.

PROMISE ME YOU WON'T

You are uncomfortable. You are both sitting on one of the sofas, but with a great difference of mien. She is curled up among the cushions—she is a supple little thing, and seems to be comfortable, but you are leaning forward with your hands clasped between your knees, which are rather ludicrously raised from the floor because the couch sags. Anyway, it is never becoming to you to argue; your face grows red and you look more clumsy than ever. She is enjoying the new sensation of seeing you ill at ease, and because of her. In the office it is so often the other way around.

"But I don't think it is good for you," you are saying.

"I don't see why."

"It isn't good for anyone to be too much alone." Speak doggedly in the tone of one who has made the same remark at intervals all his life.

"Oh no," she protests. "I think it depends a lot on the person. I think everybody ought to have privacy. I don't see how the people here do without it, I really don't. I have to keep my shades down all the time, living in the basement like this. Even at that the girls are always coming in—a couple of people have keys."

"What?" you cry. She laughs.

"Just the girls, silly." You are somewhat confused and she feels abashed at having called you silly. It sounds too intimate, somehow. Move your feet uneasily and knit your brows in an effort to say tactfully just what you think.

"I don't like it. You need your rest. It's all right for a while but pretty soon it'll react on you. I don't understand you girls. You don't use one of these studios for anything, you're at the office all day anyway. You don't even save so much money." She laughs and then looks at you inquisitively.

"Really, you're taking it awfully hard. What's the matter? What's worrying you?"

"I don't know.... I just don't like it all."

"I know," she says, teasingly. "You didn't like the dinner. I know you didn't. Confess you didn't!"

"I'm not worrying about the dinner," you say hastily. "I don't care much about what I eat; it was only that the place didn't look clean. You never eat their stew or anything like that, do you?"

She answers sarcastically, "It's terribly nice of you to worry so much about me...." and you flush.

"Now, don't talk like that. Please don't."

"No, honestly, I mean it. I wrote Mother that she certainly wouldn't worry so much about me if she could hear how you're always lecturing me. I'm so afraid you'll walk into the office some day when it's raining and bellow, 'Miss Merrill, where are your rubbers?'"

This is better. Relax and laugh loudly. "Better look out, or I will!"

In the relaxed atmosphere of the joke you suddenly find enough courage to lean over the necessary few inches and put a hand on her shoulder, rubbing your cheek against hers for a second.

She is discomposed, although it is not very surprising after all.

"Here!" she protests, breathlessly. "Stop that! Why did you do that?"

"Sorry. But I wanted to."

"Well...." She is at a loss. She giggles and says, "And besides, you need a shave."

"Yeah. Sorry.... Another thing, I think probably you don't have very good people hanging around here."

"How can you tell? You haven't met anyone but Mary. You said she has nice ankles."

"Did I?" you ask, surprised. "Maybe I did. But I don't like women to cut their hair so short. That's one of the things I like about you, by the way. You

13. PROMISE ME YOU WON'T

may be in business and all that, but you haven't lost your femininity." Close your hand over hers where it lies on the cushion.

"That's not a compliment these days."

Shake your head violently. "Don't kid yourself. We really like the same type all the time, we men. You know, you worry me a lot in the office."

"Really? How?"

"Well, because———" Stop and knit your brows. You are trying very hard to express yourself sincerely. "In the office you treat everybody so darned nice…. I mean you're a great little mixer and it's fine for business, but doesn't anyone ever misunderstand? You know what I mean, don't you?"

She looks at you with a startled expression which changes to a hurt one. She falters. "You mean I don't act—do I act too fast? I'm awfully sorry. I thought that———"

Pat her hand furiously. "No, no! You act fine! I didn't mean to criticize you at all, but you know how men are. Listen here." You raise her chin and look at her eyes searchingly. "If anybody tries to put anything over on you I want you to come and tell me about it. I want to be a friend of yours."

"Thank you," she says softly, "I consider you a friend now."

"That's mighty nice of you. It makes me feel fine. You're such a decent kid, and I don't think you know a thing about life."

"Oh," she cries pettishly, "there you go again! I guess I can take care of myself!"

"Yes, but this is what worries me. I don't like the idea of these long-haired kids filling your mind up with free love theories and all that. You're an intelligent kid too, and youngsters like you are sort of experimental."

"But———"

"Wait a minute. You don't know; you can't tell now how you might feel one of these days. It's dangerous, this stuff. You may not know it, but we're a pretty rotten lot. Most men are out for what they can get."

"I think that's horrid; to be worrying like that all the time. I don't want to have to be on my guard all the time."

"Of course you don't. Of course you don't."

"And as for my being silly, I think you ought to realize that I have a little common sense. Or even if you don't think so, don't you think that I have some ideals?"

"That's the way I like to hear you talk. Maybe you think I'm being sort of nosey, but I can't help worrying about you. You're awfully sweet."

She has a fleeting moment of misgiving. This isn't the way a boss ought to be talking. But you are very kind to be so worried…. "Yes," she says, flippantly, "If I were Miss Moser you wouldn't take so much trouble, I guess."

"Well, nobody's likely to bother her, at her age. I do want to keep an eye on you. You don't look so efficient as you are; a man's likely to forget what a swell little secretary you are when he looks at you. Here, isn't this more comfortable?" Put your arm under her head. The room is very still and cozy. "Listen."

"What?" she says, comfortably.

"I want to ask you something."

"What?"

"I want to ask you to promise me something."

"Well?"

"Promise me that—that you won't let anyone...." Silence. "Hm-m-m?"

"If you think that I need to promise——"

Kiss her (to silence her). Then—"You know I don't mistrust you," you say, gruffly, "but I get worried. Won't you promise?"

"Sure," she answers. The silence of the room flows over you again, and it too holds a promise.

14. AH, WHAT IS LIFE?

TYPE:
Middle-aged, plump, precious. The kind of man who goes to teas and avoids unpleasant situations, but does nothing else. Small white hands and shiny lips.

SUBJECT:
Ardent adolescent, seventeen or so. Quick to find Beauty in a poem or an automobile, an eclair or a man.

APPARATUS:
1 Long low living room
4 Bookcases
20 Ashtrays, all different
1 Tea set

REMARKS:
Before attempting this experiment, read Freud on the connection between artistic appreciation and the reproductive instinct. This is an indirect method and calls for careful handling.

AH, WHAT IS LIFE?
"But don't you think," says Cynthia, "that as a rule we lose sight of that quality? It's no use trying to cultivate a soul."

"No," you answer lazily, wisely, "I should be distinctly annoyed with anyone who plucked my sleeve when I was busy, no matter how many hyacinths he might wish to call to my attention. No, the true sense of beauty thrives only where it is not watched. Unfortunately it becomes self-conscious far too easily. And then, of course, one becomes articulate ... after he has lost his reason for speech.... Ah," with a wistful little smile, "I'm mawkish today. You mustn't start me off, my dear. Look at the tender color on the sky and stop thinking. I'll read to you. Something decadent. Here.

White clouds are in the sky.
Blue shadows of the hills
Between us two must lie.
The road is rough and far.
Deep fords between us are.
I pray you not to die."

She says nothing; she does not even sigh. She looks at you and waits.

"Ah, youth, youth! The beautiful simplicity, the terrible complexity of inexperience. Straight, clean…. I have lost the gift. I cannot read that poetry. Give me the sophisticated; the keen irony of Eliot; the ponderous exaltation of the negroes…."

"Of course," she says, in a rather chastened tone. "But I still like music in my poetry. Don't you still like the Hymn to Proserpine—or don't you remember? 'From too much love of living——'"

Take it up and finish it smoothly, with an indulgent smile but giving it full value and a dying fall.

"I'll wager," you say, smiling, "that you know every word of Rupert Brooke."

She blushes. "That isn't fair! You know all about me!"

"It isn't hard," you say. "I was so much like you at your age, you see. There, I'll stop teasing. Let's talk about something else. Look at my greatest treasure, down there in the corner of the bookshelf. No, not that. That's a Blake. It's a nice little thing, but you'll get yourself dusty. There it is. First edition. Did you ever see one before?"

She is not sure which of the two volumes you are speaking of; the Beardsley Salome or the new Contes Drolatique. She is exquisitely careful and reverent with both of them; opening one on her lap and looking at it for a minute. She doesn't stay interested very long, however. She wants to listen.

"Just toys, of course," you say. "I'm ridiculously dependent on material things like that. The more delicate the edifice the more firm the foundation, I've decided. No——" as she starts to speak, with an ardent gasp—"I know you don't agree with me. The tree of Job and a savorless crust in the desert for you; with a voluptuous purple sunset in piquant contrast…."

"That's cruel of you!" she cries.

"Yes, it is. You mustn't be so sensitive. I like to tease you; then I'm always sorry. I don't know why I do it. Yes I do. It's really that I envy—bitterly—your ideal asceticism. So you mustn't pay any attention to me. I'm pink and old and plump and I don't know what I'm talking about. Go on home and call up your—Boy Friend, isn't that what you call him? Go on out and dance, little pagan. Dance and stop worrying. I'll worry for you. I'll burn incense and think of you, and pray for myself."

She ignores this nobly. "Incense? Where do you burn it? In front of that gold thing there?"

"Thing? My dear!" Speak gravely. "Tread softly: he hates you enough already. He is old and you are young: he is only half divine, and you…."

"I do believe," she giggles, "that you're really afraid of him!"

"Of course I am. But I shall overthrow him soon, out of my own strength. I'm going to be a Papist."

"Honestly?"

"Yes, it has the true aestheticism of aristocracy."

14. AH, WHAT IS LIFE?

She sighs. "You say things so wonderfully. You're absolutely continental."

"Dear child! You shall have some tea for that. My very special flower tea. Sit there so I can see you while I fix it. No, don't read that book. It isn't for little girls."

She promptly begins to read it. Bring out the table and connect the little electric range for hot water. The long shadowy room grows darker and outside the automobiles begin to turn on their lights.

"There now," you say. "Take this, if you like the cup."

"Oh, isn't it lovely! I think it's so nice that your cups are all different. Mother simply insists on having everything in sets, even our books."

Groan in agony, and you smile at each other, feeling cozy and superior. She eats one piece of cinnamon toast and glances wistfully at another, but decides against it.

"We'll leave the things for Maria in the morning," you explain. "Then it's perfect. Now where is that poem you were going to show me?"

"Oh, I can't," she cries. "It's dreadful!"

"Don't be silly, please," you beg.

"All right. I think you'd better read it yourself. Don't you hate to have people read your things?" Miserably, she pretends to look at a book while you read.

"But this is lovely!" you cry. "Here, I'll read it aloud.

At night I close my window
And through the glass I see
Dancing in the moonlight
A silver tree.
I dream about it all night long,
But in the early dawn
With dream and sleep and part of youth
The tree is gone.

Lovely! It has a freshness, a sincerity...."

"Oh, honestly? You're just saying it!"

You answer severely, "I'm not speaking now as a friend, my dear. I'm speaking as a critic."

"Then could you tell me how to improve it?" she begs. "It needs—something." You both think deeply.

"M-m-m," say in a judicial tone. "Let's see. One thing I'd do, perhaps—but no. Perhaps I'd transpose the words in the penultimate line and then it would read 'sleep and dream' instead of 'dream and sleep.' Otherwise the thing is perfect."

She nods vigorously. "Yes, you're very right. I see it now. Thank you so much. It's wonderful of you to bother."

"Bother? It's no bother. You don't realize—you can't realize what your youth does for me. Almost, my dear, almost I forget my figure and my horrible hair and—well, never mind. It doesn't matter. What does anything matter in the clearness of your voice and the gladness of your face?"

She sits very still as you pass your hand gently over her hair. Her shining eyes are fixed on something invisible that hovers in the room just over your head. Mystery, or the answer to all mystery? A new confidence, a new belief, are coming into her life. It is like being kissed in a dream; wondering a little, but detached; peaceful in an even exaltation.

The room grows darker and the swish of the motors make a faint pulsing music from the boulevard. There comes an evening coolness. She is thinking; her cheeks are flushed. The bright colors of the books on the shelf are smothered in darkness, but you can see that her cheeks are flushed. She has forgotten where she is, who she is, everything. Very softly, taking elaborate care to avoid the tea-table, go over to the door and lock it.

15. A MAN MY AGE

TYPE:
Married, more than forty-five, discontented and not very attractive at first glance.
SUBJECT:
Warm-hearted but somewhat slow and heavy in her thought-processes. Has many women friends. Various men sometimes wonder why they didn't marry her when it was possible. A good sport, but very respectable.
APPARATUS:
1 Chesterfield divan, very comfortable but dusty
1 Fireplace
1 Stack of Wood
1 Fire, roaring
REMARKS:
The married man has an advantage. He has had training; he is actually as one might say trained, or tamed. He is forbidden by law and thus he acquires glamour and romance.
A MAN MY AGE
"I love this," she says.
"So do I," you answer. "I'm sorry the place is so messy. I didn't notice until you walked in. That nigger never cleans up unless Emma keeps after her. I don't know what'll happen now."
"Well, when Emma gets back it'll be all right," she says.
Glance at her in some surprise. "But I thought you knew about that," you protest. "Emma isn't coming back, you know."
"No? Oh...." She is fearfully embarrassed. She feels a little angry. "Of course I didn't know. You didn't tell me. How should I know?"
"But of course I thought—— Why do you suppose she didn't tell you? I thought you were the first one she told. I'm so sorry. I'd better——"
"You'd better tell me about it," says Barbara. "She didn't really have a chance, the last time I saw her. My sister had lunch with us and went down to the station too."
"Sure, that explains it. Why, it was this way. We went up to the cottage in June, and she went to Bedford after that. We came to an agreement after

we left the city; I don't know just when. It took a long time. We changed our minds a lot."

"I should think so," she murmurs.

"Well," you go on, "it's been three months anyway, off and on. I guess we've just been really separated for a couple of weeks. It seems longer because of that adjustment period. She can do what she likes about the divorce; I've left it up to her. I told her to do what she thought best. Emma knows how to go about business and all that. Of course I'll agree to anything."

"You mean you've definitely decided——" Her voice is incredulous.

"Nothing's definite. But if you mean is it all over, yes. We agree on that, absolutely. Are you really so surprised?"

She thinks about it for a minute. "No," she decides, "not really. I noticed something. That night you had the party before we all went to the beach, I knew there was something wrong. But I had no idea…. Do you mind talking about it? Some people might."

Shake your head and laugh. "Certainly not. It hasn't been particularly painful, you see. You're one of the family anyway. Why should I mind?"

"I'm glad you feel that way about it," she says. "Of course I'm frightfully interested."

"Then it wouldn't bore you?"

"No," she says. She maintains a reserved attitude; politely interested. Sit back against the cushions and draw a deep breath.

"I want to be fair to Emma. I guess the fault was on both sides. I can't help remembering that after all, it was my idea that we get married. I remember it perfectly well: I had to argue with her. You mustn't think that I'm trying to whine about it." Smile at her rather sadly and whimsically.

"Ben, you know I don't," she cries.

"I don't know. Naturally I feel a little defensive. After all, I suppose you're on her side. I met you through her."

"Don't be silly. I just want to hear the truth. You're both my friends."

"That's what I wanted you to say, Barbara." The fire crackles comfortably. "Well, anyway, there it is. I don't know just how it happened. My fault, I suppose, but I refuse to feel guilty. I'm awful. I keep wondering why in hell I wanted to get married. I remember in a very vague and impersonal sort of way that she was pretty."

"Oh yes," she says eagerly. "Wasn't she pretty?"

"I don't know when all the trouble did start. I can't even figure it out. I don't know that I want to." Kick the flaming log.

"I think I can understand," she says slowly. "Of course I'm trying to be impartial, and Emma's one of my best friends, but I think that I do understand."

"Yes, you would understand," you answer. "There's one thing, though, that I'd like to tell you. I mean this: I do feel badly about it. I may not

15. A MAN MY AGE

act that way, but I do. It's been awfully hard on her. Don't think I haven't worried."

"You know, Ben, there's something I want to say." She sits up and folds her hands.

"Go ahead."

"Well, I haven't any right to say it, but I'm going to. I think that your trouble is, you worry too much."

"Me? Worry? Barbara, you're a nut!"

"I mean it. You think too much for her and everybody else. You pretend to be absolutely careless about everyone else, but you aren't. You can't get along like that; it isn't nature. It doesn't work out."

"Maybe." Frown at the fire. "Maybe. But what about her? She can't face things alone, you know. I'm sorry if I'm talking too much, but this is serious. Now we're started on a long subject. She simply can't do it. She isn't fitted for it. You must know that. You're an old friend of hers."

"Ben, how long have you been worrying like this about other people?"

"You're asking me how old I am!" you cry in dismay. "It isn't polite of you. I'm much too old for you to be wasting your time on my domestic troubles. You'll have to be satisfied with that. I won't tell you."

"I know how old you are. Emma told me when you were married. What's the matter with you? You're not old."

Get up and fix the fire to hide your pleasure.

"You're a sweet girl, Barbara. You've always been the only one of Emma's friends I had any use for. You're the only mutual friend we've ever had, I may say."

"Thanks, Ben. Anyway I'm flattered that you've told me so much."

"I wonder why I did. There's something about you that makes people talk. What is it?"

"Is there?"

"I think it must be that you're so honest, yourself. How do you happen to be so honest?"

"Why not? Most people are."

"No they aren't. Most women aren't. Emma wasn't. You knew that, didn't you?"

She considers it. "Oh, Emma didn't lie."

"Not directly. But Emma was essentially feminine; essentially evasive. You aren't."

"No," she admits, serenely.

The silence is becoming dangerous.

"Heavens!" she cries, suddenly. "I had no idea it was so late. I'll have to go."

"Wait until this log burns down," you suggest. "You surely aren't in such a hurry as all that. I'm afraid to be left alone. You've no idea how lonely an old man can get in a few minutes."

She laughs. "Well, I'll wait for a little. I hate to leave the fire. I'm getting old, too."

"Besides, you're a very busy person and I haven't really seen you all year. I think I've just realized how nice an evening like this could be. I think I've been waiting for this for days, without knowing it. I feel much better, really."

"I'm so glad," she says, seriously. "I've been a little bit blue, myself."

"You?" Incredulous. "I didn't know that you ever felt blue. What on earth were you blue about?"

"Oh, I'm such a useless person. I don't really do a damned thing. I've been thinking all day about things. And then when I see people like you and Emma having your troubles too—you were two people that I always thought of as being fulfilled, sort of. Now it seems to take away my last hope. Emma's my best friend, in a way, and now I find that you've both been very unhappy. It just fits in with everything else."

"You make me feel very guilty. I didn't want to depress you. I've been selfish."

"Oh, I was depressed already! No, you made me feel a little better, somehow."

"My dear," you say softly, "I do think you're taking it harder than I did. You've been telling me that I am too sympathetic, too."

"Well, it isn't just sympathy, perhaps," she says. "I was applying everything to myself."

"You think too much," you advise. "Stop thinking too hard about life. It never does any good. I know. I've done it too."

She is silent, and you begin again. "Barbara," taking her hand, "I want to give you some advice. I'm a lot older than you are and I think we're something alike. Don't you?"

"Well, yes," she says. "I have thought so."

"There are things a lot more important than little married relationships such as Emma's and mine. It's those things that really fill our lives, Barbara. For instance this talk I've had with you tonight means much more to me than any little love-affair. Don't you see what I mean?",

"Yes, I think so. We are friends, aren't we? Real friends."

"That's it. Here we are talking about this and that, and it's the most pleasant thing I've ever done. It's been a quiet civilized sort of time. Not everyone is capable of such a relationship. Don't you think we're a little ahead of the rest of them?"

She watches you and nods. "Yes, you're right."

Pat her hand. "You're an adorable child. The fire needs fixing. Just a minute."

"Oh, Ben!" she cries. "I have to go. Really. Don't fix it for me."

"Too late," sitting down again. "It's caught already. You'll have to wait a while longer."

She hesitates, looking at her wrist watch. "I oughtn't."

"Just a minute, dearest."

"Well, all right." She smiles at you. Catch your breath and then seize her in your arms.

"Oh Barbara! I do love you so, much!"

16. GONNA BE NICE?

TYPE:
City product, bad complexion but quick brain. Too impetuous for steady success.
SUBJECT:
Very young, very canny. Always hunts in pairs with others of her kind. Fond of chewing-gum and marcel waves.
APPARATUS:
1 automobile, touring type
1 companion
REMARKS:
A very limited method. There are many girls who would refuse to be subjects on such short notice under any circumstances whatever. But for those who are at all willing to aid in the experiment, this lesson should do as well as any.
GONNA BE NICE?
The crowds walk much more slowly on the streets in the evening. They aren't going anywhere; they haven't anything to do. For the same reason, perhaps, the autos seem to loiter as they pass the people on the pavements. They aren't going anywhere much. They're open to suggestion. Two by two the people walk; sometimes there are more; hardly ever are there less.

Large groups of young boys all too young to smoke; all smoking. Little groups of girls looking in the shop windows. Two girls especially, looking in the windows for lack of something better to do. Not exactly discontented, not consciously bored. Just looking. Just walking.

Among the cars is one that goes a little more slowly even than the rest. It is a middle-aged Dodge touring car with two boys in the front seat, very much on the lookout. They pass the two little girls and call out experimentally cheerful and more or less expectant of rebuff. One of the girls looks oblivious and yet slightly more scornful, but the other smiles a little. On the chance of success, the driver of the car goes around the block and passes them again. As he disappears around the corner for the second time, the scornful girl suddenly relaxes.

"If they come back again, let's," she says.

"Sure," says the other, indulgently. "They look all right."

A third time you call to them, and this time the girls stop walking and stand waiting as the car comes to a halt. The boy who is not driving jumps out and opens the back door. Ruthie, the scornful girl, steps in while Rosie gets into the front seat, and the car speeds away. It has not taken a moment.

"Well, where to?" you call from the back seat.

"I don't care," answers Bill. "What do you say?" he adds, turning to Rosie. "Got any favorite drives?"

"No," says Rosie, "I don't know much about the roads. What do you say, Ruthie?"

"Ruthie. It's a nice name," you say, and put your arm around the owner of it. She does not cuddle down, but sits up more swiftly than before.

"Why," she says, with a surprising decision, "the Jamestown road is pretty good as far as the fence with the vine on it. When you get that far you better turn back."

Bill turns the car toward the Jamestown road and settles down to driving, while Rosie curls up in the other corner of the seat and watches him. They both wait for the other one to start talking. At last——

"Gee," she says admiringly, "you sure go fast. You ought to be careful in the city. I got a cousin who was pinched yesterday."

"Yeah? Never mind; I know the cop on this road. It ain't so much the speed, it's what they call reckless driving they pinch you for. If a fellow knows his business you can be pretty sure they leave him alone. They don't care for no speed limits."

"I guess you're right," says Rosie.

"Why not?" you ask. "You don't have to hit me in the Adam's apple, neither." Ruthie does not answer, but looks out of the car with unmitigated scorn. Pull your arm away from her shoulder and sulk. The car bowls merrily over the rough road until it reaches the fence with the vines, and it shows no signs of slowing up. Rosie does not seem to notice, but Ruthie calls promptly from the back seat:

"It's time to turn back."

"Oh, yeah," says Bill over his shoulder. He stops the car, pulls on the brake, and in a very business-like manner he puts his arm around Rosie and slumps down in the seat to a position where he can watch the sky without craning his neck. Ruthie waits a minute uncertainly, then turns away from you and stares with dignity at the fence and the field beyond it.

In the front seat the couple manage to find a comfortable position as close together as possible. You glance at them, then back at your own girl.

"What you so crabby about?" you ask, aggrieved. "I ain't pulled any rough stuff. What do you think I am? You don't have to be afraid."

"Well, what do you think I am?" she demands. "You guys think that just because a girl comes for a ride...."

"Oh, can it," wearily. "Of course I don't."

16. GONNA BE NICE?

"Well...." she says, as you pull her over to him, "It really is getting sort of late."

"It's early," you say. She shakes her head, looking very uncomfortable hunched up against your shoulder. She suffers it for a while, but her mind is elsewhere.

"We have to go back," she suddenly announces. "Right away. Rosie, we have to go back."

"Yeah, that's right," Rosie assents, cheerfully. It all seems to be the same to Rosie. "We gotta go, Bill."

"Oh, wait a minute, can't you?" you say, exasperated. "It isn't late at all."

Adamant, your girl shakes her head and looks expectantly at the driver. You and Bill glance at each other and raise your eyebrows.

"You wait a minute," you say, meaningly, and Bill obligingly turns back and looks at the scenery in front of the car.

"Now listen," you say. "You're a long ways from home."

"Yeah?" says Ruth, calmly.

"Yep. See? Well, are you gonna be nice?"

She compresses her lips. "You bet I'm gonna be nice, big boy. Come on, Rosie," and she opens the door of the car and steps out to the road. Rose hesitates, looking inquiringly at Bill. She reaches tentatively for the door-catch.

Ruthie stamps her foot. "Come ON, Rosie. You ain't got any sense at all."

Rose hesitates no longer, but steps hastily out of her seat.

"Wait a minute," you call together, as your respective maidens start down the road toward town.

"We were only kidding," says Bill. "Come on back."

"All right," assents Rosie, joyfully and with obvious relief, and she climbs back to her place. Ruth follows more slowly. Nor does she deign to look at you until you are back in the city street where you met.

"Now where?" calls Bill. "Want some chop suey?"

"We want to get out just where we got in," she answers with chilly sweetness. As the car stops—"Come on, Rosie," she says. And as Rose trots faithfully after her, with only one wistful backward glance———

"Nice ride," she adds, over her shoulder.

You and Bill look at each other.

"You weren't so smart," says Bill.

17. LIFE IS SHORT

TYPE:
Philosophical and attractive. Really sincere in his ideas; somewhat the missionary type but better looking.
SUBJECT:
Almost any girl without too much mentality. Pretty and rather spoiled because of it.
APPARATUS:
1 Canoe
REMARKS:
This lesson was an old one when Herrick counseled his young friends to gather rosebuds while it was still possible.
LIFE IS SHORT
(They are in a canoe, and the sun has just set, leaving behind it streaks of fading pink in the sky and on the water. It is spring, and the woods in the distance are losing their starkness. There is no breeze; the air is full of a premature languor that is not quite warmth. She lies half-prone, with her hand trailing in the lake; and he paddles slowly, watching her most of the time.)
She: Ooh, the water's terribly cold. Have you gone swimming this spring?
You: Went in last week. But I was sorry. It's colder than it looks from the diving-board. I was awfully surprised—it's such a shock.
She: I wanted to try it today, it looked so warm. But I guess I'll wait a while. Last year, all summer, we just lived in our suits. My suit was never dry. Don't you love to swim? It's my favorite exercise.
You: I think I like sailing better. It's so fast.
She: Then you ought to like ice-boating. It's much faster.
You: No. It's too noisy. Fast things ought to be quiet. That's the trouble with flying in a machine. It isn't really flying unless you have wings. That must be the best feeling in the world. Flying in a storm….
She: I wouldn't want the storm. I haven't that much pep. Swimming's nice because you can lie around so much.
You: You're a lazy little thing, aren't you?
She: That's what they say at home.

You: I like it. I hate these girls who are always trying to be better than you are in everything. They're usually funny-looking, too. If they were pretty they wouldn't worry so much about beating people.

She: You have such old-fashioned ideas. Well, I guess you're right. I like to be waited on. People do things for me. I like it…. Oh, look at that cloud. It's getting rougher than it was—We must be drifting out.

You: Yes, it goes faster than you'd think. There's a little wind blowing up. (Starts paddling fast.)

She: Going anywhere?

You: Well, I know a place that is pretty sheltered. Say, I'm getting cold up here. Do you mind if I get down there with you?

She: No, that's all right.

(You start to step over the intervening bar, and the canoe sways dangerously. She screams loudly.)

She: Look OUT! You're tipping us!

You: (Laughing and settling down next to her) Gosh, what a funny squeal! I never tip canoes: don't you know that? Have a cigarette.

She: Thanks. The lake looks pretty, doesn't it? Just in this light.

You: Did you ever notice, it's never the same. Look at that boat way over there.

She: It looks so little.

You: It's funny. This is a little lake, but that boat looks tiny on it just the same.

She: (Uncomprehending) Yes.

You: I mean we're really awfully small when you think about things. Stars and things. Look at that star there——

She: First one! I'll wish on it. (She closes her eyes.)

You: It's a little bit of a star, but I wonder what it thinks about us. Probably it doesn't even know you're wishing on it. Just think, it can't even see us. Just a little spot of light.

She: I don't like to feel that way. I want to be seen.

You: I think it's a good feeling to know that I don't matter so much. I always remember it when I'm worried about an exam. It's a bad habit, though, because if you start remembering it too soon you don't even bother to study.

She: I shouldn't think anybody would. I never feel that way unless I need sleep. I hate it; feeling that way.

You: You're too practical. I think I have more fun my way. (Smile at her and flick your cigarette into the water.)

She: I don't see that. I don't worry, anyway.

You: No, but look. You take exams seriously and spend all your time studying or fixing clothes or something. Something really important. Don't you?

17. LIFE IS SHORT

She: Yes. Only the thing I worry about most is dancing. That's important too.

You: Well, look at it my way. Look how long the world has been going on without me and my exams. Look how long it will go on, probably, after I'm dead. Look how short life is anyway.

She: Yes....

You: Well, I just do what I like. Studying isn't one of those things, see? Nobody really likes to study.

She: I do.

You: No you don't. You don't really like to keep your stockings mended, or your hair curled. You just like the feeling afterwards that you did what you should have done. Isn't it true? Well, then, if someone hadn't taught you to like that feeling you wouldn't be doing those things. Now, the things I like, I wasn't taught. I like to eat. Nobody ever had to tell me to do that. I like to sleep, and swim, and sail, and kiss girls, just because it's fun. Itself. No reason for it, except that if I keep on this way I can go on doing these things and having fun until I die. I won't want to die, then.

She: Well, I think you're the lazy one. Where would we all be?...

You: I don't know, but wherever it was we'd probably like it just as well. (Lean over suddenly and kiss her.)

She: Don't do that!

You: Why not? (Kiss her again.)

She: Stop. Why should I?

You: There you go again, asking questions. Why? Because it's fun.

She: I don't think it's so much fun.

You: You haven't really tried. Give me a chance. (Kiss her again.) Now what do you think of it?

She: Not very much. Let's go on talking instead.

You: That's queer. You always tell me I talk too much. I think you don't mind this so much as you say.

She: You want to think so. I just don't see why it's so wonderful. I couldn't possibly rave the way you do, that's all.

You: I don't rave. It's because I know what I'm talking about and you don't.

She: You have a lot of nerve.

You: Well, you can see for yourself that you're no judge. You don't know anything about it. You said so yourself. And besides, if you're going to do so much talking about it you're wasting time until you know something.

She: It's no use trying to argue with you, is it? I'm going home.

You: Now you're just running away because you lost the argument. It isn't my fault. You said you wanted me to talk. All right; I'll stop talking. (Kiss her.)

She: No, I didn't mean that. Stop. Please stop.

You: No, I won't. You need convincing.

She: But....

You: You mustn't talk for five minutes. That's reasonable, isn't it? Five minutes!

She: All right. (Seven minutes elapse.) The five minutes must be up.

You: What did you say?

She: The five minutes are over.

You: What of it? What's five minutes when the whole evening will be over in a short time? All of the evenings will be over some day. And you're quarreling about five minutes. Oh, stop talking!

She: But.... Oh, all right.

18. I'D HAVE SAID YOU WERE FROM NEW YORK

TYPE:
Traveling salesman, always just a little lonely and overjoyed at a chance to talk or make any human contact whatever.
SUBJECT:
Inexperienced traveller in a state of high excitement and anticipation. At a rare stage of impressionability.
APPARATUS:
1 Pullman car
REMARKS:
This method is extremely specialized, suited only to travelers. On terra firma both protagonists are different people entirely, who would be scandalized at actions which seem perfectly plausible on the train.
I'D HAVE SAID YOU WERE FROM NEW YORK
There's really nothing else to do on train journeys. Reading on the train gives you a headache; after three hours scenery should never have been invented. And as for that green plush…. If you have an acquaintance on the train and talk yourself out with him you will never want to see him again…. Bridge? But that is our story.

Sometimes on trains or boats there are signs like this: "Beware the Professional Gambler; He is Smarter Than You." This is romantic. But it is not the type of romance which appeals to most young women, and as a rule they ignore the signs and play bridge. On the chance that you do not know your Dreiser, I shall attempt to describe the requisite technique.

Carrie is sitting forlornly in her chair in the Pullman, with a closed Red Book in her lap. Sunk in the crack of the chair is a discarded College Comics. She doesn't want to buy another magazine; she wishes the man with the cap would stop bothering her with Eskimo Pies and perfume, and bananas and paper-backed novels. The train smells sooty. Large hard balls of soot keep falling into her lap. Outside the window is the same yellowed field that she has been watching all day. It twists and presents various corners to the passing train, but it's the same field just the same, with the same wheat lining up into orderly ranks that fall apart into chaos as the train passes on. Twenty more hours and nothing left to think about....

You walk down the aisle, staggering as the train sways. She looks at you idly. You are tall and skinny, and when she sees that you are beginning to get bald, she loses interest. At the same time you see her. You have been looking for her ever since she passed through the club car on her way from lunch: you like them small and blonde and young when there are no tall and blonde and snappy ones. Stop by her chair and smile at her.

"Would you like to join a party at bridge, if I can start a game?" you ask. Her first impulse is to refuse; not from caution, but from inertia. It's the same feeling that made her turn down the man with the cap on his last journey when she really wanted a bar of Hershey's. But as she shakes her head she changes her mind. Bridge! Something to do!

"Why—yes, I guess so." And she giggles a little, from shyness.

"Good! I'll get someone else and be back in a minute." But you return with bad tidings. Everyone else is already playing.

"I guess we got the idea too late," you announce, sitting down in the next seat. "I wish I'd thought of it before. There was an old fellow in the back that asked me this morning, but he was getting off at Chicago. Isn't that where you got on? How far are you going?"

"Colorado. I'm going to get off this train at La Junta." Whistle.

"You have pretty near as long a ride as I have. I go clear across. Tiresome, isn't it? I ought to be used to it, but I never am, somehow."

"What do you do?"

"Furniture. Wholesale furniture. I'm traveling for a firm in Tucson; Robinson and Company. Have you ever been there?"

"Oh, no; this is my first trip West."

"It's a nice town, but hot right now. I'm lucky to be away. Just had a letter from my—my sister and she says the heat is unbearable. Unbearable."

She murmurs sympathetically and looks back at the wheat, while you remember that at times you talk too much about yourself. Ah, well then....

"If it isn't too personal—what part of the country do you hail from?"

"Illinois. Darien. It's just a little town. I'm going out to Colorado to visit and maybe I'm going to stay. If I can get a job teaching and if I like the country, I mean."

"Really? Now, I'd have said you were from New York."

There is a pleased little silence.

"Why, what a funny idea. Why should you think I'm from New York?"

"Oh, I don't know. A man in my business gets so he can spot people pretty quickly, and he can't exactly tell how, nine times out of ten."

"Kind of second nature?"

18. I'D HAVE SAID YOU WERE FROM NEW YORK

"Yes, second nature. I don't know just why I did think you were from New York. Your clothes, or perhaps the way you talk. Or the way you know how to take care of yourself."

"How can you tell anything about that?"

"Oh, that's easy. A man can always tell. You can take care of yourself."

She blushes and remembers that she is all alone on this train.

"Well," slightly raising your voice, "I do like New York. It looks pretty good when you've been out in the sticks for a couple of months."

"I'll bet it does."

"Yes, there's no place like New York for shows. I wouldn't like to live there, but it's a good place to visit. My—my mother used to live there, and I never could see how she stood it as long as she did."

She answers with animation. "Oh, but the little towns get so dull! There just isn't anything to do out in the country."

"Nothing to do? Why, gee, what's the matter with fishing? Two weeks a year isn't enough fishing for me!"

"But of course you're a man."

"Sure, that's right. A man feels different. I admit I don't understand women, and I bet I'm as bright as the next one. There's not a man alive can understand a woman."

"Well, maybe you're right."

"Isn't it time to eat? Let's go on in and see. Will you have dinner with me?"

"Why—I don't know——"

"What's the harm?"

No nice girl will admit the possibility of harm. She ignores your remark, therefore, by rising and starting for the dining car. It is seven cars away, and some of the long passages are difficult to manage without staggering from side to side. Hold her elbow in a firm grasp, squeezing it as she stumbles against you, and laugh a good deal. You are much better friends when you reach the diner.

She looks out of the window at the sweeping darkness and you watch her and she knows it. The speed of the train and the feeling of not belonging anywhere are very exciting. What will Colorado be like? What is it all about anyway? No one in the train is a real person; they are all simply part of an adventure, like the armies and mobs in the background of a moving picture. Even the man across the table—isn't he simply part of it too? The most exciting part? A personification of the whole thing, the whole waiting world.... I'd have said you were from New York.... You can take care of yourself.... I certainly can.... She smiles at you suddenly, defiantly, gayly. "What were you thinking about?"

"Oh, I don't know. The future, I guess."

"I thought so. Let's drink to it." Hold up your water glass. "To your future, and may it include me."

She laughs again, recklessly. Lean over the table.

"Will it, kid? Will it?"

"Oh——how do I know? I'm no fortune teller." Again she turns to the window. There are no fields to be seen now, but the stars look very large. Stars and darkness and the train going somewhere—somewhere—somewhere. And that man looking at her and appreciating all her expressions and knowing that he doesn't understand her; wondering about her....

"Now what are you thinking about?"

But she'll never tell you. You'll always wonder about the girl you met on the train for a few minutes. Ships that pass in the night. It's exciting to be going somewhere.

She doesn't want any more ice cream. Go back to her chair and when someone asks you to play bridge refuse without even consulting her. No matter. Stare out of the window.

"You know, it's a funny thing. This has been a much better day than I expected."

"How do you mean?"

"Oh, you know. I thought it would be just the same. You can imagine, riding on trains day in, day out."

"Yes, I can imagine."

"I'm glad you got on at Chicago, that's all. You won't be sore at me for saying so? I've got to say what I think, to you."

She can feel just how it must be. Your profile looks so tired.

Turn to her suddenly. "I'm talking like a crazy person. Do you think I'm crazy?"

"Of course I don't."

Settle back again. "Good. I'm not really, but I guess most people would think so."

"Why should they?"

"Talking like this to a girl I just met on the train."

"Talking like what? You haven't said anything." She is really bewildered.

"Haven't I?" Look at her again, quickly. "You know, that's a queer thing. I thought I had. I thought I'd said lots of things. Do you ever have that feeling?"

"Oh—that. Yes."

"Well, I know what I'm going to say, right now. You'll probably be mad at me."

"What is it?"

"I think you're a darned good sport."

"Why? You don't know. You don't know anything about me at all."

"Sure I do. I'm not dumb. I've been watching you all day and I guess I can tell as well as the next one. Do you know what I think about you?"

"How should I?"

18. I'D HAVE SAID YOU WERE FROM NEW YORK

"I think probably you're awfully nice." Put your hand over hers. "I know you are. You're all excited, aren't you?"

"What makes you say that?"

"You're shaking. What's the matter? Scared of me?" Your hand tightens.

"Oh, no." She is annoyed with herself. It's hard on the nerves, sitting in a train all day. Almost time to go to bed, she thinks—the porter has started at the other end of the car; his head is immersed in the upper berth in the corner.

"It's getting late," you say, understanding her. She nods and thinks with a new terror of arriving in a strange town. Nervous.

"I'm sorry," you add. There is another silence. Some perverse shyness keeps her from saying anything. It is almost as if, against her own will, she waits for something fateful. But say no more. Pat her hand and settle back, looking up at the top of the car.

Slowly, followed by a mysterious growth of little green cabins, the porter approaches you, slamming down chair-covers, manipulating linen.

Sit up with a new briskness.

"I'm going to the smoker," you announce. "But listen, I'm not going to say good-bye." She looks at you and waits. Her tongue won't move; is it curiosity? Nervous....

"I'm coming in to say good-night," say, your eyes fixed on hers. "I have a book to lend you. So long." Rise, and then put your hand over hers again. She simply stares at you.

"You're a nice kid," you observe, and walk away.

Slowly she stands and picks up her suitcase as the porter reaches her chair in his constructive progress. Slowly she walks down the aisle to the Ladies' Room. A sudden flush of thought as she gets there—she drops the bag and looks into the mirror, horror-stricken. Why didn't she say something? What should she do now? Then as she thinks, she feels better. He's simply coming to say good-night. Sure, he'll probably try to kiss her, but—oh, well, stop thinking. Just the same she'll wear her dressing gown to bed; no use giving him ideas. Everything seems so different on a train; if it would stop making a noise and let you think straight.... Ships that pass in the night. What's the difference?

19. SHE LOVED ME FOR THE DANGERS

TYPE:
Restless wanderer, appearing at intervals of four or six years to sit on the hearthstones of his old college friends and look wistful. At the slightest chance of attaining a hearthstone of his own he dives back into the wilderness.
SUBJECT:
Any co-ed
APPARATUS:
1 Automobile
1 Head of gray hair, above one of these
never fading bronzed faces.
1 Precise accent.
REMARKS:
The advanced student will favor this method, since it transcends the makeshifts and awkwardness of all other human experiments and utilizes a policy which has heretofore been monopolized by divinity (see Introduction). Here the student seduces by means of imagination. It is the culmination of our efforts; the ultimate degree of subtlety.
SHE LOVED ME FOR THE DANGERS
It is a dull afternoon in the sorority house and Dorothy is trying to make up her mind to study; but she isn't having much success. In fact, the idea is so unattractive that she doesn't waste more than half a minute trying. Everybody has gone to the last game of the season across the river, and Dot didn't go because she has used up all her week-ends. Oh, well ... Sunday afternoon and five hours before her date. Nothing left to read. Washed her hair yesterday—you mustn't do that more than once a week. Manicured her nails before lunch. Plucked her eyebrows, darned her stockings—oh, bother Sunday afternoon. And there is a theme due on Tuesday, but that's a long time and anyway you write better themes at the last minute. Oh, glory, there's the phone. What if just once it could be someone unexpected?
"Miss Dormer? This is Donald Banks, from Los Angeles. I have a letter

for you from Genevieve Reed. When I left I mentioned that I might be coming through here and she thought——"

"Why, any friend of Jen's—why, of course. Can't you come over?"

"I'd very much like to. When would it be convenient?"

"Any time this afternoon. I think I'm busy tonight, but if you'd like to come over now or pretty soon it would be all right."

Well! Oh, well, he'll probably be a mess. Jen never mentioned him. Haven't heard from Jen lately, though. It wouldn't be like her to send up a wet smack.

No, you aren't a wet smack at first glance, anyway. Interesting looking. Lean and distinguished; something like Lewis Stone, if not quite so tall. How funny of you to think that the sitting-room is really a place to sit—surely no one else spent all afternoon on that horse-hair sofa since the Dean of Women was a pup. If you were one of the boys you'd know enough to suggest going out. But it is rather fun at that.

"Oh, you mustn't think," she protests, "that you have to go just because it's so quiet. We're allowed to have visitors indefinitely on Sunday."

Laugh. "You're tired, though. I remember Sunday afternoon at school from my own experience. Thank you, and—I may see you quite soon again? Not only, I assure you, because my time in your city is so limited."

Ooo, what a funny way to talk! "Certainly." It is queer, how hard it is to keep from getting an accent like that too, while she talks to him. "Yes, I'd like to see you again before you leave. It doesn't happen to be a very—busy time for me just now."

"How fortunate! I don't want to interfere with your studies. Can't we have dinner this evening?"

"Oh—why—yes, thank you, I'd like to. At six-thirty? Good-bye."

Oh, well, Tom ought to excuse her for an out-of-town friend. That is perfectly legitimate.

"Hello. Alpha Belt house? Is that Tom? Well, listen, Tom? I hope you won't be perfectly furious because I really can't help it, but it's this way——"

A co-ed is a well-protected person, in spite of what may be read in the newspapers about her freedom. She is so hemmed in by public opinion—not the opinion of the outside world, but that of her own public, the campus—that it is with a distinct sense of guilt that she associates with anyone so foreign as an out-of-town visitor, be his appearance ever so distinguished. Not that Dorothy isn't thrilled as well as apprehensive. If she dared, she would even have dined in the roseate and familiar publicity of Ye Kandy Shoppe, stared at by her friends and causing a poorly concealed flurry of gossip. But you would be puzzled by Ye Kandy Shoppe, and perhaps dissatisfied with the food. That is why you proceed solemnly through the menu of the Imperial Hotel Dining-room, sherbet-on-the-side and all, surrounded by the younger married set of the town, with an occasional drummer or a professor's party.

19. SHE LOVED ME FOR THE DANGERS

"Well, yes, I see that you know Genevieve quite well," you are saying. "Much better than I do. It's perhaps the only fault that I can find with my work—the lack of real social contact. Going and coming as I do, I must resign myself to being the picturesque figure; oft forgotten. Interesting, perhaps, but so occasionally!" Smile.

"But doesn't your work keep you in one place at a time pretty much?" asks Dorothy. "I thought it took at least six years at a time to build bridges. Surely there are people there—in Abyssinia, or wherever you're going next?"

"People? My dear child, you've been going to the movies. The natives are really dark—much more so than you seem to suspect. Of course once in a while you do find people, and if they are people at all, you understand, they mean much more to you than they would here, at home. That mode of life has given me a distressingly intense way of taking my friends, I find. You children with your great circles of acquaintances wouldn't understand my attitude."

"I might," she says, eagerly. "Once I spent a summer camping—in Maine—with just three other people, and I certainly was glad to get back to town. I was so sick of them!"

"Yes, that might give you some idea of it. But don't misunderstand me. I wouldn't give it up for anything. After all in the face of certain things, what do people matter? I give you my word—" here your face grows intent as you finger a fork; you seem to have forgotten Dorothy and the dining-room "—a man gets pretty close to the fundamental reason for things, out there. So close that he is perilously near to discovery. What keeps him from going farther? Sometimes he goes too far. Sometimes a boy is sent back home just for going too far—for discovering, or thinking he has discovered.... Fever? Insanity? Truth?"

Dorothy shivers. The tawdry dining-room is forgotten in dark imaginings. Slimy twisted vegetation, slow streams of oily water, houses built on stilts, lifted from the swamp.... Or the monotonous sun of the desert; the undulating, glaring floor of sand with one heroic little clump of tents....

"Would you care to dance?" You have come out of it. She smiles, rather late, and nods. You dance the way they do in those places in Europe, she thinks—slow and romantic, not hopping all over, like Tom.

"When do you start back again?"

"Well, I'm not sure. I won't know until I get back to New York. They keep these things quiet, of course—international policy, I might say." For the first time, your smile is for her; a personal thing. "I have a very definite regret that my visit is so short. It's an unaccustomed feeling. The last time I saw civilization—let's see, it must have been four years ago—I was positively glad to go back. Where do they keep you young girls? Are you always at school? Ah, well—thank education for our salvation!"

It is difficult to imagine you at a movie, she thinks. You go, however, and sit through a news weekly, a very old domestic comedy, at which you laugh quite surprisingly hard, and half a problem picture before you give it up.

"I say," you suddenly announce, "stupid of me not to have thought of it before. Simply driving somewhere would be better than this. Or have you a rule about cars and that sort of thing?"

"I suppose we must have, but no one ever pays any attention to it."

You must drive a good way before the Sunday traffic is at last left behind.

"You drive well for not being used to the city," she ventures.

"It's good fun," you explain. "Much more dangerous than the life out there. And you mean to say that you do a lot of driving? In streets like those in town? Brave girl!"

Safe from the eyes of any university official, she takes a cigarette. Your silence and proximity are very thrilling; there will be a lot to tell the room mate when she gets back. Or perhaps it would be better not to say too much—to act as if this sort of out-of-town friend is to be expected from a background like Dorothy's. She is rather different than the usual co-ed, anyway, she thinks comfortably. More interesting friends, on the whole. Of course these little boys are all right when you have nothing else....

Stop the car on the edge of the Hawk Bluff, which in the sober light of common day looks out over a not-very-far-down golf course, but which now hangs over mysterious abysses.

"Dorothy," you say.

It has come at last; she knows it and turns to you with the fatal feeling of one for whom circumstance has been too strong. And then nothing happens for a minute.

"You are a lovely child," you say. Then, very quickly, draw her to you and kiss her on the brow. And then drive home through the quiet night. Anyway, it is quiet until you reach town and the boisterous returning students.

Home again, an hour before she has to be. Stand in the light-speckled gloom of the verandah and say farewell.

"So very, very nice of Jen. I'll never forget it. Something to remember when I go back.... Lovely child."

And without even another kiss on the brow you are gone.

Does Dorothy call up the Alpha Delt house to arrange for a malted before she goes to bed? Or does she go to her room and sit there in the dark, thinking?

She goes to her room quite thoroughly, as it were, seduced. After all, this is the most subtle method of them all.

BIBLIOGRAPHY

Mrs. D. M. Craik, John Halifax Gentleman. (Everyman).
Russell, A Year in a Yawl. (Doubleday Doran).
Malinowski, Sex and Repression in Savage Society. (Harcourt Brace).
E. Osgood, Cupid Scores a Touchdown. (French).
MacCuaig and Clark, Games Worth Playing. (Longmans).
W. J. D. Mead, The Energies of Men. (Dutton).
Collinson, Life and Laughter 'Midst the Cannibals. (Button).
Hamlin Garland, Back Trailers from the Middle Borders. (Macmillan).
R. J. T. Bell, An Elementary Treatise on Curve Tracing. (Macmillan).
M. E. Bottomley, The Design of Small Properties. (Macmillan).
Louisa May Alcott, Little Women. (Macmillan).
Leonard Merrick, One Man's View. (Dutton).
Mary B. Grubb, When Mother Lets Us Make Gifts. (Dodd Mead).
Anon, Mother Goose. (Macauley).
Elinor Glyn, Three Weeks. (Macaulay).
Margaret Kennedy, A Long Week-End. (Doubleday Doran).
Lina and A. B. Beard, American Girl's Handbook. How to Amuse Yourself and Others. (Gregg Pub. Co.).
Hord and Ely, How to Get a Good Position. (Gregg Pub. Co.).
"Pansy," An Interrupted Night. (Lippincott).
Robert Browning, Love Among the Ruins. (Macmillan).
R. S. Carroll, Our Nervous Friends, Illustrating the Mastery of Nervousness. (Macmillan).
Edgar Allan Loew, Electrical Power and Transmission; Principles of Design and Performance. (McGraw).
Laird and Lee, Laird and Lee Diary and Time Saver. (Macmillan).
S. C. Johnson, Peeps at Postage Stamps. (Macmillan).
Harry Castlemon, Frank on a Gunboat. (Donohue).
C. Askins, Wing and Trap Shooting. (Macmillan).
Herbert Adams, The Empty Bed, Rogues Fall Out. (Lippincott).
J. H. C. Fabre, Life and Love of the Insect. (Macmillan).
"   Life of the Scorpion. (Dodd).
H. M. Lothrop, The Five Little Peppers. (Lothrop).

George Birtwhistle, New Quantum Mechanics. (Macmillan).
Cocke, Old Mammy Tales from Dixie Land. (Dutton).
Bernardin de St. Pierre, Paul et Virginie. (William Morrow).
Aristophanes, The Birds. (William Morrow).
J. M. Barry, Peter Pan. (William Morrow).
Dean Swift, Gulliver's Travels. (William Morrow).
Margaret Mead, Coming of Age in Samoa. (William Morrow).
Etienne Rabaud, How Animals Find Their Way About. (Harcourt Brace).